The THINK Series

THINK about
Nuclear Arms Control

The THINK Series' Editors: William N. Thorndike, Jr.,
Ramsey R. Walker

Stylistic editor: Martha Goodale, Mary Pavlik
Fact checker: Catherine Monk
Reading consultants: Anne-Marie Longo, Paula Sable

Jacket design: Joyce C. Weston
Text design: Joyce C. Weston
Photo research: Diane Hamilton
Graphs: Jill Thompson
Jacket illustration: Tom Hughes
Text illustrations: Jeff Danziger
Appendix A written by J. B. Schramm

The editors would like to thank the many teachers, librarians, and students that assisted in putting together the THINK Series. It would be impossible to thank everybody; however, we would especially like to thank the following people: John Buckey, Betty Carter, Jim Davis, Mike Hartoonian, Tedd Levy, David Mallery, Mike Printz, Bill Polk, Mary Tabor, Ellen Ramsey.

THINK about

Nuclear Arms Control

Understanding the Arms Race

Richard Smoke

The THINK Series

Walker and Company
720 Fifth Ave.
New York City, NY 10019

First published in the United States of America in 1988 by the Walker Publishing Company, Inc.

Published simultaneously in Canada by Thomas Allen & Son Canada, Limited, Markham, Ontario.

Library of Congress Cataloging-in-Publication Data

Smoke, Richard.
Think about the nuclear arms race and arms control.

(The Think series)
Bibliography: p.
Includes index.
Summary: Discusses the nuclear arms race, its historical background, technological ramifications, and impact on contemporary life.
1. Nuclear arms control--United States--Juvenile literature. 2. Arms race--United States--Juvenile literature. 3. Nuclear arms control--Soviet Union --Juvenile literature. 4. Arms race--Soviet Union --Juvenile literature.
[1. Nuclear arms control. 2. Nuclear warfare. 3. Arms race] I. Title. II. Series.
JX1974.7.S487 1987 327.1'74 87-23110
ISBN 0-8027-6761-3
ISBN 0-8027-6762-1 (pbk.)

Printed in the United States of America

10 9 8 7 6 5 4 3 2 1

Figures 1, 4, courtesy of the Signal Corps, U.S. Army; Figures 6, 7, 8, 10, 13, 17, 20, 22, 24, 26 official photos courtesy of the U.S. Air Force; Figure 16 courtesy of the Library of Congress; Figures 19, 21 courtesy of the National Archives: Nixon Project.

CONTENTS

INTRODUCTION

Practically everyone seems to feel that the nuclear arms race is one of the biggest problems facing humanity today. Top governmental officials, religious leaders, executives of corporations, heads of labor unions, and presidents of universities—almost all of them say that the possibility of nuclear war is the most important danger we face.

For instance, in 1986 the *Christian Science Monitor,* one of the most respected newspapers in America, asked some of the best-known leaders and thinkers in the United States: "What should be on America's agenda as the nation enters the twenty-first century?" In some ways, these national leaders differed in their answers. One raised the problem of the world's overpopulation; one brought up the environment. Yet they all agreed that the risk of nuclear war was the most important challenge of all. Preventing a nuclear war was at the top of everyone's list of what we must do.

In fact, this problem is so big and so serious that some people don't like to think about it at all. Some people try to avoid talking about it. Thinking or talking about it makes them feel anxious. Also, some people feel that the nuclear arms race is too complicated to understand.

But trying to run away from a problem really just makes it seem bigger! And of course nothing can be solved that way. The way to solve a problem is to face it and master it.

Furthermore, some aspects of the nuclear arms race are complicated, although others are not. To try to understand *all* aspects of it can get very complicated indeed. There are many kinds of missiles, bombers, and nuclear weapons. How each kind of weapon relates to all the others can be complex. But the *overall* meaning of the nuclear arms race is not so complicated.

The purpose of this book is to provide you with a broad understanding of the nuclear arms race and to familiarize you with some of the major issues and events that have shaped it. You will learn about ways that people have tried to control the arms race and also the language of the arms race, so that you can read more about it later.

This Book's Approach

The nuclear arms race is, in a sense, like a movie. You can't understand a movie very well if you see only the last part of it. And you can't understand the nuclear arms race very well if you look only at the most recent part of it—what is going on now and what has been going on in the last few years. Just as in a movie, you can only understand it well if you see it from the beginning.

That is what this book does. It shows you the "movie" from the beginning.

The nuclear arms race began more than forty years ago, so that is where this book starts. The first chapter tells you about the beginning, and each succeeding chapter brings you closer to the present. The last two chapters discuss the present and the future.

Don't let yourself get worried as you read. This

problem is a big one, but there *has* never been a nuclear war, and a great many people think there won't be one—especially if we do the right things in the years to come.

1 The Nuclear Arms Race Begins

When did the nuclear age begin?
Could atomic weapons be controlled?
When did the Cold War begin?
What did the atomic monopoly mean?

On the morning of August 6, 1945, a single American airplane flew over the Japanese city of Hiroshima. This was very unusual. For months, hundreds of U.S. warplanes had been flying over Japanese cities every day. The warplanes had dropped many tons of bombs on factories, military bases, and other targets. But on this morning, there was only a single airplane. It seemed so harmless that the Japanese did not even try to shoot it down.

When the airplane was over the center of Hiroshima, it dropped just one bomb. There was a blinding flash of light, much brighter than the sun; there was an enormous blast, and terrific heat. When it was over, a cloud in the shape of a mushroom rose into the sky. And where the city had been, there was nothing left but rubble. For hours after the blast, dirt and dust, sucked up into the sky by the mushroom cloud, fell back to earth in a kind of "black rain."

This was the first atomic bomb. In an instant, it had destroyed the entire city. (See Figure 1.)

Tens of thousands of people—men, women, and children—died instantly. More tens of thousands were badly wounded and died during the next few days.

Nothing like this had ever happened before in the history of mankind. Never before had an entire city been wiped out with a single blow. In Washington, President Truman announced, "Sixteen hours ago an American airplane dropped one bomb on Hiroshima . . . It is an atomic bomb. It is a harnessing of the basic power of the universe. The force from which

***Figure 1** Hiroshima was destroyed on August 6, 1945, by a single atomic bomb.*

the sun draws its powers has been loosed against those who brought war to the Far East."

WORLD WAR II ENDS

Japan and the United States had been at war ever since Japan had attacked Pearl Harbor three and a half years before. By 1945 it seemed obvious that the United States was winning, but Japan refused to surrender.

Three days after Hiroshima, the United States dropped a second atomic bomb. This time the target was the Japanese city of Nagasaki. It too was completely destroyed in a moment. Some 40,000 people died instantly and another 35,000 were so hurt that they died within months.

The Japanese assumed that the U.S. could go on to destroy all of their cities this way. Five days after the Nagasaki bomb, the Japanese surrendered.

World War II was finally over. It had been the worst war in history. More people, about forty million, had been killed in World War II than had died in any other war. Far more Americans had been killed in this war than in any of America's previous wars.

Throughout the United States, and nearly everywhere else, people were jubilant that the war was over. They could live at peace once again. They no longer had to fear that their brothers or fathers would be killed fighting, and they no longer had to fear that some enemy would overrun their country.

The fact that the war had ended was more important to nearly everyone than *how* the war had ended. Having peace and not having to live in fear was what people cared about most. The invention of a terrible new weapon seemed less important. For the first time in a long time, Americans would be able to live normal lives again.

ABOLISHING THE BOMB?

In the years that followed, whenever people in the United States thought about the atomic bomb, they felt glad that America was the only country with the technology to build it. How to build the bomb was an American secret. American scientists, with help from some European scientists, had discovered how to build a bomb, and after the war the United States kept this technology to itself.

In Washington, government officials who were making plans for the future realized that the technology could not be kept secret forever. Scientists in other countries would eventually figure out how to build bombs, too, so other nations would eventually have their own bombs. U.S. officials worried about a world in which many different countries had bombs and about how peace would be maintained in the future.

To try to ensure peace, the United States government developed a plan. It was called the Baruch Plan, named for the man who presented the plan to the world, Bernard Baruch. Under the Baruch Plan, the United States would make a generous offer. The U.S. would give up all its atomic bombs. All existing bombs would be dismantled as inspectors from all over the world watched. In exchange for this, the whole world would agree that *no one* would ever build a bomb again. The United States would never build another one, and no other country would ever build one.

To prevent any nation from building bombs secretly, the U.S. proposed that all countries join in creating a special worldwide police force. This police force would oversee all laboratories and factories in which work on an atomic bomb could possibly be done.

In presenting the U.S. plan to the United Nations Baruch said, among other things:

> We are here to make a choice . . . If we fail, then we have damned every man to be the slave of fear. . . . Science has torn from nature a secret so vast in its potentialities that our minds cower from the terror it creates. . . . We must answer the world's longing for peace and security. In that desire the United States shares ardently and hopefully. . . . She stands ready to proscribe and destroy this instrument . . . if the world will join in a pact to that end.

Many people around the world liked the Baruch Plan, and the governments of many countries said they would agree to it. Most Americans liked it too, even though it meant dismantling all our atomic bombs. Most Americans were willing to give up the U.S. bombs as long as no other country was able to build them.

The Baruch Plan had one flaw. The United States could give up all its bombs, but it could not give up the *knowledge* of how to build an atomic bomb. Once U.S. scientists had discovered that, there was no way for them to forget it again. What the scientists knew, they knew.

Under the Baruch Plan, the special worldwide police would prevent any other country from ever acquiring the ability to build bombs. This would give the United States an enormous advantage over the other countries of the world. If it ever looked as though there might be another war, the United States would be able to build new atomic bombs quickly, and no other country would be able to.

Nobody could think of a way to get around this problem. Inevitably, the United States would always have an enormous advantage over everyone else.

Some countries would not agree that the United States should be in this privileged position forever. The most significant country to disagree was the Soviet Union. The Soviets said no to the Baruch Plan.

The Soviets came up with a plan of their own, which they offered the world. But this plan had an even worse flaw. It gave the U.S.S.R. and every country veto power over where the special police could go. According to the Soviet plan, the Soviets could simply stop the police from inspecting atomic laboratories and factories in the Soviet Union itself. The Soviets could build bombs secretly, and the police would have no way to find out.

Very few countries agreed to this plan, and certainly the United States did not. The result was a stalemate. The Soviets would not agree to the Baruch Plan, and the United States would not agree to the Soviet plan. Neither plan was adopted.

The attempt to stop atomic bombs from being built, at a time when only a few existed, had failed.

THE "COLD WAR"

The disagreement concerning atomic bombs was not the only disagreement between the United States and the Soviet Union at this time. The two countries also had a bitter disagreement about what was happening in Eastern Europe.

During World War II, the U.S. and the Soviet Union had cooperated in defeating Nazi Germany. American and British troops had attacked Nazi Germany from the west, and Soviet troops had attacked from the east. Together, they had defeated the Germans in 1945. (See Figure 2.)

Then the cooperation ended.

The Americans and the British withdrew all their troops from Europe and brought them home. Only a few soldiers were kept in West Germany to assure that a new democratic West German government was set up. But the Soviets kept a very large army, known as the **Red Army,** in East Germany and in almost all the countries in Eastern Europe that they had overrun on their way to Germany.

The Soviets did not allow the East Germans—nor the Poles, Hungarians, or other Eastern Europeans—

Figure 2 During World War II, the Soviet Union and the United States cooperated to defeat the Nazis. Twenty million Soviets were killed when the Nazis moved into the U.S.S.R. in World War II, increasing the Soviet fear of invasion.

to create democratic governments. The Soviets did not allow any of these countries to control their own affairs. Instead, the Soviets set up "puppet" governments in these countries. A **puppet government** is one that does what another country orders. The Eastern European people couldn't resist because the Soviet Red Army was everywhere.

The United States, Britain, France, and the other free countries of the West were grief-stricken and angry. America had just fought a long and terrible war to save Europe from the tyranny of the Nazis. Now another tyranny was taking over Eastern Europe.

The United States and the other Western countries did everything they could do, short of starting another war, to prevent the Soviets from keeping control over Eastern Europe. Many strong protests were sent to the Soviet Union. But the Soviets would not budge.

Relations between the Soviet Union and the West became tense and hostile. No one wanted another war. No one wanted millions of soldiers fighting and millions of deaths. But the Western countries vowed that they would never forget the Soviet tyranny over the Eastern Europeans, who numbered almost a hundred million people.

The state of tense, hostile relations continued, and soon people named this situation the **Cold War.** The term "Cold War" came into use in 1947, and was used almost everywhere in the West until the 1960s to describe relations with the U.S.S.R. Thereafter, use of the term faded, although some people still use it.

TWO THEORIES TO EXPLAIN SOVIET MOTIVES

Why did the Soviets take forcible control of Eastern Europe? Why have they kept this tight control right down to today? Even now, we in the West are not sure why. The Soviet government does not reveal the real reasons why it does things.

In the West, there are two main theories to explain it. Some people believe one, and some the other. Some people believe that there is truth in each of them.

One theory suggests that the Soviets *want* to take over more and more countries and that, in the long run, they want to rule the whole world. At the end of World War II, the Soviets had a perfect opportunity to increase their power and territory. Their army was in control of half of Europe. Why withdraw? They simply took advantage of their opportunity.

The second theory proposes that the Soviets are basically *afraid*. To understand this, you have to know a little about Russian history.

Russia does not have immense oceans on both sides of it the way America does. Instead, there have always been other powerful countries near Russia's borders. (Imagine America's position if, instead of the Pacific Ocean, there were powerful countries just to our west.)

Over the last five centuries, Russia has been invaded from its westward side, not once but time after time. Just since 1800, there have been three huge invasions. Each time the invaders were thrown back, but only after tremendous suffering and losses.

The third, and worst, of these was the Nazi invasion in World War II. Twenty million Soviets—soldiers and civilians both—died between 1941 and 1945. A large and important part of the Soviet Union was overrun. (Imagine how Americans might feel if during World War II the Nazis had landed on the continent and conquered all of the United States as far as the Mississippi. Imagine that we had to reconquer our own territory at the cost of twenty million American lives.)

The second theory suggests that at the end of World War II, the Soviets decided to prevent another invasion by erecting defenses to the west of their own territory. They kept a big army stationed there, and they forced the little countries on their western border to serve as a buffer. If there was ever another attack, the war would be fought in this buffer zone, and not on the Soviets' own territory.

These are the two theories that explain why the Soviets took over Eastern Europe after World War II. The first theory suggests that the Soviets are basically aggressive. They seized Eastern Europe to increase their power and territory. The second theory suggests that the Soviets are basically defensive. They took control of Eastern Europe because they thought it was necessary to their future defense. Even today, the West cannot be sure just how much truth there is to each theory.

THE THREAT TO THE WEST

No matter what the explanation is, we know what events actually took place. The Soviets created puppet governments throughout Eastern Europe and used the Red Army to make sure there could be no resistance. This began just as World War II was ending. By 1948, Soviet control of Eastern Europe was complete and unshakeable. It continues to this day.

The United States and the democratic countries of Western Europe were not only grief-stricken and angry about this, but they were also worried. They felt a threat to the West, too.

By a year after World War II ended, all of the Western democracies, including the United States, had greatly reduced their armies. Almost no troops remained in Western Europe. What was to prevent the Soviets from simply marching into Western Europe and taking it over? There was no military force to stop them.

This worried American and other Western officials more and more. After all, the Soviets had proved that they were willing to seize control of whole nations. They were doing just that in Eastern Europe. Why should they stop there? There were no Western armies to speak of that would halt them if they should decide to march west.

In those days, there was a popular phrase that many Americans repeated because it seemed to sum up the situation. The phrase went like this: "All the Russians will need is shoes" to march all the way to the Atlantic Ocean. In other words, the Soviet Army wouldn't even have to fight to take over the small countries between East Germany and the Atlantic Ocean.

THE WEST—BOTH WEAK AND STRONG

In the late 1940s, the West felt both weak and strong. The West's weakness was that it had no way to stop the Soviet army from invading Western Europe. Yet the strength of the West lay in the fact that the United States was the only country able to build the atomic bomb. After the failure of the Baruch Plan, the U.S. had built more bombs. With the beginning of the "Cold War," building bombs seemed the only prudent thing to do.

As relations between the United States and the U.S.S.R. became more and more strained, the possibility of another war loomed. Just after World War II, Americans did not feel that atomic bombs were terribly important because the world was at peace, but now they were taking on great significance.

At first, it was only a few officials in Washington who realized this because it was their job to think ahead this way. But gradually, Americans woke up to the fact that it was *important* that the United States had atomic bombs and no one else did.

SECURITY FROM THE BOMB

Because the U.S. was the only country capable of building bombs, the United States had what was called an **atomic monopoly.** Atomic bombs were so enormously powerful that the U.S. monopoly gave America a tremendous advantage should another war be waged. (See Figure 3.) In fact, the U.S. would have so great an advantage that there simply was no question who would win the war.

If there was a war between the United States and the Soviet Union, the U.S. would be able to destroy Soviet cities, just as the U.S. had destroyed two Japanese cities. In case the Soviets were tempted to

***Figure 3** In 1949, the U.S. still held an atomic monopoly. People began to fear another war as tensions increased between the U.S.S.R. and the U.S.*

march into Western Europe, American officials warned them that the U.S. would retaliate. Soviet cities would be destroyed with atomic bombs if there was a new war.

Of course, this kind of threat made the Soviets angry and helped to worsen the Cold War state of hostility and tension. At the same time, the American threat reassured the Western European democratic nations. Now that the Soviets knew what the consequence would be if they attacked, an attack was very unlikely. The Western Europeans would not have to be so concerned about a Soviet invasion.

To reassure the Western European democracies further, the United States and Canada created a military alliance with them. The alliance was given the name "North Atlantic Treaty Organization," or **NATO** for short. This alliance was a formal, legally binding commitment. Thirteen countries in Western Europe joined NATO, and each member pledged to fight if any one of them was attacked.

SUMMARY

The destruction of Hiroshima and Nagasaki with atomic bombs quickly ended World War II. Through the Baruch Plan, the United States proposed to give up its bombs, but it could not give up the knowledge of how to make them, and the plan failed. The Soviets proposed their own plan, but it also failed because the world would have had no way to assure that the Soviets were living up to it.

After World War II, the Soviets seized control of Eastern Europe; even today people in the West are not sure how much of the Soviet motive was offensive and how much was defensive. In any case, the Red Army occupying Eastern Europe was enormous, and in the late 1940s the Western European countries had almost no armies at all.

In spite of this threat, Americans and Western Europeans still felt reasonably secure. The U.S. was the only country able to build atomic bombs and was in the process of building some. If the worst happened and a war did break out, the U.S. would win—certainly and quickly. Since everyone knew this, no one would be so foolish as to begin a war.

REVIEW QUESTIONS

1. What were the dates of the U.S. atomic bombings of Hiroshima and Nagasaki?

2. What did the Baruch Plan propose to do about the possibility of some country cheating and building bombs secretly?
3. Why were there very few American or British troops in Western Europe after the end of World War II?
4. What are the two main ideas about why the U.S.S.R. seized control of Eastern Europe after the end of World War II?
5. How many times has the U.S.S.R. been invaded from the west since the year 1800?
6. What did the phrase "All the Russians will need is shoes" mean?
7. Why did the atomic bomb seem more important by 1949 than it had seemed just after the end of World War II?
8. What does NATO stand for? Is the United States part of NATO?

PERSONALITY PROFILE

HARRY S. TRUMAN

Harry S. Truman, the thirty-third president of the United States, was born in 1884. He joined the American forces in World War I, and did so well that he was quickly promoted to the rank of captain. Returning home to Missouri after the war, he opened a clothing store, but it went under in 1921. Refusing to declare bankruptcy, he declared that he would repay every penny he owed, and he did. It took him ten years to do it.

Truman entered Missouri politics, and after holding several lower offices he ran for the U.S. Senate in 1934. Early in World War II, he proposed and then headed up a Senate committee investigating waste and fraud in the war effort. His successful investigation earned him a national reputation, and in 1944 President Franklin D. Roosevelt selected Truman as his next vice president. When Roosevelt was reelected, Truman was elected with him. FDR died in office on April 12, 1945, whereupon Truman became president and continued in that office through 1952.

As president, Truman had to make the fateful decision to drop the first atomic bomb in history. He decided to destroy Hiroshima and Nagasaki with atomic bombs because he believed (correctly, as it turned out) that doing so would end the war at once. He believed the only alternative was an American invasion of the Japanese islands, which would take a long time and mean huge American losses. He later said, "I wanted to save half a million boys on our side . . . I never lost any sleep over my decision."

2 Deterrence

When did the American monopoly end?
What is the meaning of "deterrence"?
Why is it important to be sure an attack would succeed?
When was the hydrogen bomb created?

The sense of security that Americans felt was shattered in September of 1949. At that time, the White House announced that the U.S.S.R. had tested an atomic bomb.

During World War II the Soviets had begun researching how to make an atomic bomb. After Hiroshima, they speeded up their research greatly. In only four years they discovered the secret for themselves.

In the summer of 1949 the Soviets successfully tested a bomb, but they did not tell the world what they had done. The United States' government found out about the Soviets' test and announced it.

Americans were alarmed. The U.S. atomic monopoly had been broken, and it could never be regained. What was worse, the country that had found the secret was not a friendly Western country like Britain or France. It was the Soviet Union.

People started to really worry now about the possibility of another war. The "Cold War" hostility and the tension between the West and the U.S.S.R. was not much different from the way other nations had felt toward each other in the past before they had gone to war against each other. Would the same thing happen again? Only four years since the end of World War II, people were talking about the possibility of World War III.

TWO NATIONS' BOMBS

In spite of this hostility, this situation was different from previous ones. The atomic bomb was a terrifying new weapon. Americans and Soviets alike were frightened of what a war with atomic bombs would be like.

By now the United States had built hundreds of bombs. Before long the U.S.S.R. would also have hundreds of bombs. A war in which each country dropped hundreds of bombs on the other would be a nightmare. It would be far, far worse than World War II had been.

Americans who thought about this realized that if World War III broke out, many—perhaps all—American cities would be destroyed, just the way Hiroshima and Nagasaki had been. The Soviet government also knew that if World War III broke out, Soviet cities would be destroyed the same way.

People in both countries realized that if World War III ever started, it would be infinitely worse than any war fought previously. No sane American or Soviet leader could possibly want to begin a new war, knowing that so many of his own country's cities would soon be wiped out.

DETERRENCE

This was the factor that had never existed before. The atomic bomb was such a terrible weapon that no American or Soviet who understood the situation could possibly want to fight a war.

There is a word for the situation where a country is afraid to fight a war because the result would be too terrible. The word is **deterrence.** If one country is *deterred* from starting a war, it means that the country's government would not possibly want a war because the destruction that the country would suffer would be too great.

In the years following 1945, the United States had decided to deter any Red Army invasion of Western Europe by threatening to attack the U.S.S.R. with atomic bombs if it did. After 1949, the United States also deterred any Soviet atomic attack on America by threatening to attack the U.S.S.R. with atomic bombs in reply.

Now that the Soviets were building their own bombs, they could also deter the United States. The Soviets could threaten to reply with atomic bombs if the United States attacked the Soviet Union with atomic bombs.

Deterrence, then, worked both ways. When two countries can deter each other this way, that is sometimes called **mutual deterrence.**

All this is not abstract. In the 1950s, both the United States and Soviet Union did make these threats. The U.S. and Soviet government each announced, many times, that if World War III broke out between them, it would destroy the other side with atomic bombs.

To give one example of many, Nikita Khrushchev, the chief Soviet leader in 1959, told a senior American official that the United States must not defend West Berlin by force. Khrushchev said, "If you send in tanks they will burn, and make no mistake about it. If you want war you can have it, but remember it will be your war. Our rockets will fly automatically." Later that year, Khruschev made a point of telling a group of journalists that "we could wipe all our potential enemies off the face of the earth." There are many other examples of threats back and forth.

Mutual deterrence between the United States and the Soviet Union has continued year after year, decade after decade. The United States continues today to deter any attack from the Soviets by threatening to destroy the Soviet Union. The Soviets continue to deter any attack from America by threatening to destroy the United States. Each country understands that, if it attacks, its own cities will be destroyed by the other country, just as Hiroshima and Nagasaki were.

Of course, each country makes this threat to *prevent* any attack from the other country. In other words, each country makes the threat to prevent any war starting in the first place.

This is how the United States and the Soviet Union maintain peace! Each country makes this threat, to prevent any war ever starting and hence to keep peace between them.

Many people think this is a strange and frightening way to try to maintain peace. It means trying to keep peace by threatening war—in fact by threatening the most extreme kind of destruction imaginable. (See Figure 5.) Some people don't feel that this state of affairs should even be called peace.

On the other hand, it is true that the United States and Soviet Union *haven't* fought a war against each other. Since the end of World War II, the governments of the two countries have felt hostile toward each other—sometimes more intensely, sometimes less, but always hostile. Yet they have never fought a war. Many experts believe that they probably would have before now if each country did not threaten to destroy the other in this extreme way. In other words, many experts believe that mutual deterrence has maintained peace.

Figure 5 Deterrence maintains peace by threatening war.

DELIVERING BOMBS

The fact that each side tries to maintain peace by deterring the other is the most basic single fact you will learn in this book. Unfortunately, there are many complications.

One complication is that each country has to have a reliable way of *delivering* bombs against the targets it wishes to attack. When the United States destroyed Hiroshima and Nagasaki, this was not a problem. By that time, Japan was so weak that it could not shoot down very many U.S. aircraft.

After the Cold War began, the Soviets decided that they would try to shoot down American bombers if World War III ever broke out. To do this, they built fighter aircraft and guns that shoot upward from the ground. Later they built missiles that launch from the ground, to try to intercept and destroy bombers. They also built radars, to spot and track the bombers. The combination of all these things, plus other necessary elements, is called an **air defense system.**

Naturally, this meant that the United States had to figure out a way to make sure that enough American bombers would reach and destroy all necessary targets. The U.S. had to be sure it could "penetrate" the Soviet air defense system.

In the 1950s the main way to be sure of penetration was to build more bombs and more bombers to deliver them. That way, even if some bombers were shot down by the Soviet air defense system, enough others would penetrate.

In the 1950s the U.S. built hundreds of an early model jet bomber. But before long, American engineers came up with a design for a much better bomber, called the B-52. The first B-52s were being built by 1955. Eventually, the U.S. built more than seven hundred B-52s. It turned out to be so capable a bomber that about two hundred and fifty of them are still being flown by the U.S. Air Force today. (See Figure 6.)

"ASSURED DESTRUCTION"

The only way that the United States could feel confident that deterrence was "working" was if the U.S. knew that American bombers *could* penetrate the

Figure 6 ***The B-52 was first produced in large numbers in 1955. One of the most widely used military planes, this one was photographed flying over the state of Washington in 1977.***

Soviet air defense system. The U.S. built a large number of bombers because officials in Washington wanted to feel certain that, in a war, enough bombers would penetrate.

If the U.S. was sure of this, Soviet officials would be too, and they would never start a war. If the U.S.S.R. never started a war, then we would have peace.

This is how the logic of deterrence works. If peace depends on deterrence, then maintaining peace means always maintaining deterrence. And this means *always* maintaining the ability to penetrate Soviet defenses and destroy Soviet cities. Experts use a grim phrase to describe this situation. Being sure that the U.S. can penetrate and destroy Soviet cities is called having an **assured destruction capability.** Deterrence rests on having an assured destruction capability. And in the nuclear age—so far at least—peace rests on deterrence.

In the famous movie *Dr. Strangelove,* many scenes show a U.S. Air Force base for B-52 bombers. At the entrance to the base, there is a big sign that says "Peace Is Our Profession." (See Figure 7.) These signs really did exist for many years at the entrances to U.S. Air Force bases. The Air Force was reminding people that peace rests on deterrence, and deterrence rests on the ability of the Air Force to bomb the Soviet Union.

A NEW BOMB

Being certain that the U.S. can deliver bombs against cities and other targets in the U.S.S.R. is one complication in maintaining deterrence. Another complica-

Figure 7 This sign shows one Air Force motto: Peace Is Our Profession.

tion is the fact that scientists keep making new discoveries.

For example, in 1950 scientists in both the United States and the Soviet Union discovered that it was possible to build another kind of bomb. This new bomb would be much more destructive than the bombs that destroyed Hiroshima and Nagasaki.

The old bombs worked on a principle called "fission." In those bombs, very heavy atoms (uranium or plutonium atoms) are split approximately in half, releasing tremendous energy.

Now scientists discovered that they could put together, or "fuse," two of the lightest atoms. (The lightest atoms are hydrogen atoms.) When two atoms fuse, there is an even more enormous release of energy. A bomb that works on this principle of "fusion" is called a hydrogen bomb.

Hydrogen bombs can be much more destructive than atomic bombs not only because fusion releases more energy than fission but also because there is no upper limit to how large a hydrogen bomb can be, as there is to an atomic bomb. In the 1950s and 1960s American and Soviet scientists learned how to build hydrogen bombs one thousand times more powerful than the Hiroshima and Nagasaki bombs. The first U.S. hydrogen bomb was detonated in a test in 1952.

The old bombs had an explosive power equal to about fifteen thousand tons, or fifteen *kilotons,* of the chemical TNT. A kiloton is the unit for measuring the power of an atomic bomb. The power of a hydrogen bomb is often measured in megatons. A megaton equals one million tons of TNT. A one megaton bomb is big enough to destroy even the largest city. (See Figure 8.)

NUCLEAR WEAPONS

Originally, hydrogen bombs were also called "thermonuclear" bombs. After a while people dropped the "thermo-" and started calling *all* the bombs "nuclear," whether they were atomic or hydrogen. Scientists also developed nuclear shells for big artillery guns, creating missiles that shoot down aircraft and other weapons. All these together, including the bombs, came to be called "nuclear weapons." By now, people seldom use the words "atomic" or "hydrogen" to describe these weapons.

Figure 8 This nuclear explosion was photographed in April 1954. The hydrogen bomb had been developed a few years earlier, introducing a nuclear weapon much more powerful than the one dropped on Hiroshima.

SUMMARY

The most fundamental feature of the relationship between the U.S. and the Soviet Union is *deterrence.* Ever since the early 1950s, each nation has maintained peace (from its point of view) by threatening to retaliate and wreak terrible destruction if the other country attacks. For the threat to be believed, it has to be backed by an *assured destruction capability,* meaning that the threat *can* be carried out if it has to be.

In the 1950s, both American and Soviet scientists

learned how to build fusion or hydrogen bombs. Because even the largest city could be destroyed by just one of these very powerful bombs, it would not take very many to accomplish the "assured destruction" of any nation.

REVIEW QUESTIONS

1. In what month and year did the White House announce that the Soviets had tested an atomic bomb?
2. How did the U.S. deter the U.S.S.R. from invading Western Europe in the late 1940s?
3. Why did the U.S.S.R. build an air defense system, and what did the U.S. do to be sure America could penetrate it?
4. For many years the U.S. Air Force had signs outside its bomber bases saying "Peace Is Our Profession." What did these signs mean?
5. What is the difference between "fission" and "fusion" as ways of creating an explosion?
6. Why is hydrogen used in a bomb that works by fusion?

3 The Race for Superiority

What is an "arms race"?
How did the U.S.S.R. seem to gain superiority?
What is an ICBM?
What is a "first strike capability"?

During the 1950s, while the U.S.S.R. kept improving its air defense system, the United States worked to build more B-52s to keep ahead. This is an example of the arms race. (See Figure 9.) Because the U.S.S.R. was increasing its military power, the United States felt that it had to increase *its* power also.

Of course, Soviet officials felt the same way! Because the United States was increasing its power, the Soviet Union felt it had to do the same.

The development of the hydrogen bomb by both Soviet and American scientists was another example of the arms race. Some American officials had been reluctant to build so immensely destructive a weapon, but they felt they had to, because they knew the Soviets were working on the hydrogen bomb. Meanwhile, the Soviets were working on it because they knew the United States was and because they wanted something more powerful than the American atomic bomb.

Figure 9 The arms race has continued without a stop.

In the decades since, the U.S. and the Soviet Union have often built new, more powerful weapons to "keep up with" or get ahead of the other country. The arms race has continued without a stop.

Especially in recent years, efforts have been made to halt the arms race. (You will read about these later in this book.) So far, the arms race has not been halted, although it has been reduced in intensity somewhat.

THE 1950s

Through most of the 1950s, the United States was obviously ahead of the Soviet Union in the arms race. The U.S. was building hundreds of B-52s and was confident that many of them would penetrate the Soviet air defense system in the event of war.

The Soviets, by contrast, had propeller-driven

bombers which American engineers regarded as obsolete. In fact, one kind of Soviet propeller bomber was an almost exact duplicate of a bomber the U.S. had built for use in World War II.

In the 1950s the U.S. developed its own air defense system. American experts estimated that this system would be fairly effective in shooting down Soviet bombers. But a few bombers would surely get through. Americans worried about the possibility of World War III, and they worried that Soviet bombers would succeed in reaching the U.S. with nuclear weapons. For example, in the 1950s most public schools held regular "air raid drills." When an alarm sounded, all the students would dive under their desks.

Even so, American officials were so confident of the United States' ability to destroy the U.S.S.R. that they felt sure the Soviets would never start a war. In other words, American officials were confident that deterrence was working.

Then, in 1957, the Soviets did something very dramatic.

Sputnik

On October 4, 1957, the U.S.S.R. launched the first space satellite, which was named *Sputnik.* Never before had any kind of man-made satellite orbited the earth. No nation had had the rockets to put a satellite into orbit.

Americans were very upset. This was a historic "first" of tremendous importance. The first satellite in space was something that history books would record for centuries!

Americans were used to thinking of the U.S. as the earth's leading technological nation. They were stunned that another nation had achieved this technological triumph. They were doubly upset that it was the Soviet Union, America's opponent in the Cold War, that had achieved it. In 1961, Americans were upset again when the U.S.S.R. put the first human being, Yuri Gagarin, into orbit—an achievement of equal importance.

But there was something else about *Sputnik* that was even more alarming to people who understood the arms race. The same rockets that put *Sputnik* in orbit could do something else.

ICBMs

If a rocket was powerful enough to send an artificial satellite into orbit, then it was also powerful enough to send a small nuclear bomb (called a **warhead**) to the other side of the world, very quickly. The fact that the Soviets could launch *Sputnik* meant that they had, or very soon would have, **missiles** that could attack the United States. Those missiles would carry nuclear warheads.

Americans had to learn a frightening new term: *Inter-continental Ballistic Missile,* or **ICBM** for short. (See Figure 10.) An ICBM is a missile that can deliver a warhead from one continent to another. (The word "ballistic" describes the path the warhead takes; it goes up very high and then plunges down.) This was entirely new technology, and it made bombers seem a bit old-fashioned.

The ICBM has two features that made it a very powerful new weapon. One is its speed. For a jet

Figure 10 The ICBM, developed in the late 1950s and photographed here in 1962 at Vandenberg Air Force Base in California, stepped up the arms race. While a jet bomber would take about six hours to fly from the U.S. to the Soviet Union, an ICBM could cover the same distance in about thirty minutes.

bomber to fly the distance between the U.S. and the U.S.S.R. takes at least six hours, yet an ICBM can cover the same distance in about thirty minutes.

The other feature is that, in the 1950s, an ICBM couldn't be shot down. A warhead was too small a target, moving much too fast, to shoot at. Scientists could build air defense systems that could shoot down many incoming bombers, but they didn't know how to build a system that could shoot down many incoming ICBM warheads.

THE "MISSILE GAP"

Many American experts were very worried about the Soviets building ICBMs. The United States was working on ICBMs too, but the American missiles were still under development and were not yet ready. *Sputnik* showed that the U.S.S.R. might have ICBMs soon.

When a new weapon has been built and put in place where it is ready to be used, experts say that it has been "deployed." After *Sputnik* was launched, American experts worried that the U.S.S.R. might be able to deploy ICBMs in quantity by the end of the 1950s.

American ICBMs would not be ready for deployment in any numbers until a couple of years later. This meant, experts feared, that there would be a period during which the Soviets had ICBMs deployed and the U.S. did not. Soon people coined a phrase for this situation. There would be a "missile gap" between the Soviet Union and the United States.

The missile gap would be at its worst, experts feared, from about 1960 to about 1962. After that, the

U.S. would have its own ICBMs deployed in quantity. But between 1960 and 1962, the Soviets would have *superiority*.

Officials in Washington were worried about the prospect of Soviet superiority. The U.S.S.R. had never had superiority before. Throughout the history of the arms race, the United States had always been ahead. The U.S. had had more bombs, more bombers, and more advanced military equipment of all kinds.

Many experts believed that *American* superiority had kept the Soviets from acting more aggressively in Europe and all around the world. Even despite American superiority, the Cold War was pretty tense. How much worse might the Cold War get, if superiority passed to the Soviet Union?

A SOVIET ATTACK?

The missile gap that experts foresaw for 1960–62 posed another possible problem that was even worse. Some experts feared that the U.S.S.R. might actually attack! They feared that the U.S.S.R. might start a nuclear World War III by attacking the U.S. with their ICBMs.

The reason for this fear was that the Soviets might use their ICBMs in a way that would be particularly dangerous. Supposing the Soviets attacked U.S. Air Force bases, where the B-52s were kept?

The Soviet ICBMs could arrive very fast. Perhaps the U.S. would not know that the missiles had been launched and were on the way. All the B-52s might still be parked on the runways at the American air bases when the Soviet warheads arrived.

Of course, nuclear warheads are so tremendously powerful that just one would destroy an entire air base and all the B-52s parked there. Suppose that the Soviets launched many ICBMs at the same time, aimed at *all* the Ameican B-52 bases? Perhaps all the American bases would be destroyed at the same moment!

This would be a "knockout blow." If *all* (or practically all) the U.S. B-52s were destroyed at once, then the United States would have little or nothing to strike back with.

If the U.S. could not retaliate, the Soviets would have won the important part of the war. Thereafter, they could destroy American cities whenever they pleased. They could destroy American cities with other ICBMs or they could use their bombers. No matter what they did, the U.S. could not strike back.

In fact, the Soviets might not even bother to destroy American cities. Unable to strike back, the U.S. would have to surrender. Moscow could dictate whatever terms it pleased; the United States would be defeated. In this way, the U.S.S.R. might win the entire war in less than an hour!

A "FIRST-STRIKE CAPABILITY"

This kind of special, very dangerous situation is called a first-strike capability. A first-strike capability does not mean simply the ability to strike first. Obviously either country could do that at any time. If a country has a first-strike capability, it means that that country can strike first and succeed in *disarming its opponent*. After the first strike has landed, the opponent will have so little left that it cannot penetrate the first country's defensive system.

A nation that has a first-strike capability is in a position to start a war at any time and win it at once. The opponent, after absorbing the attack, would be unable to strike back effectively.

Having a first-strike capability is the opposite of being deterred. If a country is deterred, that means it knows that if it attacks, the other side *will* be able to strike back (and therefore the first country won't dare attack in the first place). If a country has a first-strike capability, that means it knows that if it attacks, the other country will *not* be able to strike back.

THE IMMEDIATE U.S. REPONSE TO THE MISSILE GAP

You can now understand why some American experts were worried in the years just following *Sputnik*. They were afraid not only that the missile gap would give the Soviets superiority, but also that it might give the Soviets a first-strike capability. If the Soviets could win World War III in an hour, they might be tempted to attack. (See Figure 11.)

Figure 11 American officials feared that a multiple launching of Soviet ICBMs would give the U.S.S.R. a first-strike capability.

This possibility was what some U.S. experts foresaw as they looked ahead toward 1960 and 1961. But there were some steps the U.S. could take to lessen the danger, and these steps were taken.

The U.S. speeded up construction of some huge new radars. These radars could spot Soviet ICBMs, once they were launched, much earlier than any other radar, and thus give more warning time—fifteen minutes or more. Many of the B-52s were put "on alert," which meant that their crews were ready to take off in fewer than fifteen minutes.

The B-52s would be able to get airborne and away before the Soviet warheads arrived. Of course the Soviets would know this ahead of time, so they wouldn't be tempted to strike in the first place. Deterrence would be preserved.

HOW MUCH REAL DANGER?

Some American experts were not extremely concerned about the missile gap. One reason was that U.S. intelligence agencies had secret information that the Soviet Union was not, in fact, deploying very many ICBMs. Even by 1960 there were not nearly as many Soviet ICBMs as there were American B-52 bases. This meant that the U.S.S.R. did not yet have a first-strike capability. Unfortunately, the U.S. intelligence agencies were uncertain as to how many ICBMs the U.S.S.R. might deploy in the near future.

Some experts also doubted that the Soviets were so aggressive that they would *want* to begin a nuclear World War III—even if they had the good opportunity from a purely military point of view. As was explained earlier, many experts think the U.S.S.R. acts basically on defensive motives, not aggressive ones.

This is also what most Soviet citizens say. When Americans traveling in the Soviet Union ask people they meet, the Soviets nearly always say that the U.S.S.R. would never begin a world war. Most Soviets are shocked and indignant at the very idea that the U.S.S.R. would initiate a nuclear war.

But keep in mind the basic difference between the two systems. In the United States, the people control the government and elect its leaders. In the Soviet Union, the government controls the people. Knowing what the Soviet people want (regardless of how sincere they may be) does not necessarily tell us much about what the Soviet government will actually do.

SUMMARY

By the early 1950s the arms race between the U.S. and the U.S.S.R. was underway and has continued ever since. The launching of *Sputnik* destroyed Americans' confidence that the U.S. was ahead in the arms race, because *Sputnik* meant that the Soviets would soon have ICBMs. People worried that in a few years there would be a "missile gap"—a time when the U.S.S.R. had ICBMs deployed and America did not. A missile gap would mean that the Soviets had *superiority,* something they had never before had. With superiority the U.S.S.R. might become aggressive in Europe and around the world.

Even worse, some experts worried that the Soviets might actually attack the United States when they achieved a "first-strike capability." If the Soviets built enough ICBMs to strike every U.S. bomber base simultaneously, it would be possible for them to win World War III in an hour's time.

REVIEW QUESTIONS

1. Give two examples of things the U.S. or U.S.S.R. did that were part of the arms race.
2. Give an example of something often done in the United States during the 1950s that shows that Americans were aware that Soviet bombers might successfully attack the U.S.
3. What was *Sputnik,* and in which year was it launched?
4. Who was the first human being to orbit the earth, and in which year did he do it?
5. What were the two features of an ICBM that made it a very powerful new weapon?
6. Name two things the U.S. did to reduce the danger that the U.S.S.R. might attack during the time that the "missile gap" was expected.

4 The Cuban Missile Crisis

Why was the "Cuban Missile Crisis" such a threat to our national security?
How did President Kennedy respond to this threat?
Why did the Soviets make such a bold move by installing missiles so close to U.S. territory?

Just after 7:00 P.M. on the evening of Monday, October 22, 1962, millions of Americans sat with their eyes riveted to their television sets. The president of the United States was addressing the American people. This special address had been announced only hours before. The president told the American people that a dangerous crisis had erupted.

The president was John F. Kennedy. In October 1962, President Kennedy faced the most difficult and dangerous crisis that any American president has ever faced, before or since. Experts agree that this crisis posed a very real danger of nuclear war.

The President told the American public that the Soviets had begun to place nuclear missiles in Cuba.

This was a brand new threat and a serious one. Cuba was only ninety miles from the American coast. A large number of Soviet missiles in Cuba would threaten the United States in a way the Soviets had never been able to before.

Fidel Castro had seized power in Cuba in 1959. (See Figure 12.) Soon he revealed that he was a Communist, and he allied Cuba with the U.S.S.R. Thereafter, the United States warned the Soviets many times that the U.S. would not tolerate any kind of Soviet nuclear weapons being brought so close to American shores.

The Soviet government promised over and over that it would never send nuclear weapons to Cuba. But then, in 1962, the leaders in Moscow secretly sent Soviet missiles to Cuba by ship. Even while doing this, Soviet leaders continued to promise the U.S. that they would never do it. Obviously, these promises were lies. (See Figure 13.)

By putting their missiles into Cuba secretly while saying that they weren't, the Soviets hoped to create a great surprise. They hoped that the U.S. wouldn't find out until the missiles were deployed and ready

***Figure 12** The Soviets, with the support of Cuba's leader, Fidel Castro, wanted to put missiles aimed at the U.S. in Cuba, only ninety miles from the American border.*

***Figure 13** This photo, taken by the U.S. Air Force in early November 1962, shows missile equipment at the Mariel Port Facility in Cuba.*

to launch. The Soviets hoped that the U.S. would not dare destroy the missiles once they were deployed.

Once the U.S. was forced to accept Soviet missiles in Cuba the Soviets planned to send more and more missiles. Soon there would be so many missiles in Cuba that every part of America could be attacked and destroyed from an island only ninety miles away.

The Soviet plan almost worked, but not quite. U.S. intelligence agencies *did* find out that the Soviets were putting missiles in Cuba. They learned about it before—though not long before—the missiles were deployed and ready to launch.

This information was brought to President Kennedy's attention at once. Kennedy realized he had to act before the Soviet missiles could be made ready. The President immediately assembled a group of top officials and other advisors to help him decide what to do.

The first plan that Kennedy and his advisors considered was to order the U.S. Air Force to attack and destroy the missiles. The Air Force would use **conventional weapons** (ones that are not nuclear) in this attack. An air attack with conventional weapons was dangerous, however, because Soviet troops, not Cubans, were putting the missiles in place. Soviet leaders in Moscow would be very angry if Soviet troops were killed in an American attack.

Then the U.S. intelligence agencies learned that it would be several days before the Soviet missiles could be made ready. This information gave the president more time.

Kennedy decided to try another plan first. He would not yet order the Air Force to attack the missiles with conventional weapons. Instead, he would publicly demand that the Soviet government remove all the missiles at once.

Kennedy would also order the U.S. Navy to blockade Cuba. In other words, he would have the Navy halt and search all ships headed toward Cuba. A blockade would stop any more Soviet missile equipment from getting to Cuba. This is the plan that was carried out, starting Wednesday morning, October 24, 1962.

THE PRESIDENT ANNOUNCES THE U.S. DECISION

The president went on television on Monday evening to explain the situation to the American people and to announce his plan. The U.S. would take no immediate action that would lead to anyone being killed. But Kennedy demanded that the Soviets remove the missiles in Cuba at once and forever.

In his television address, Kennedy explained how the Soviets had been warned many times not to place nuclear weapons in Cuba. He explained how the Soviets had lied. He explained how great the threat would be if Cuba, so close by, became an island full of Soviet missiles. He explained that there would be no fighting and no one killed if the Soviets did not try to force their way through the Navy's blockade, and if they removed the missiles that were already in Cuba.

President Kennedy and his advisors hoped that the Soviets would choose to take the peaceful way out of the crisis. If they removed the missiles and sent no more, the United States would take no further action. The crisis would be over.

But the president was also prepared for the possibility that the Soviets would refuse his demands. They might go ahead and finish deploying the missiles in Cuba. The Soviets might instruct their ships to force their way through the Navy blockade.

The president ordered the Navy to sink, if necessary, any ships approaching Cuba that did not stop to be searched. He told the Air Force to prepare to attack the missiles in Cuba. If the Soviets refused to remove the missiles, the president would then fall back to his first plan. He would order the Air Force to attack, rather than allow those missiles to be made ready to launch.

At the end of his television address, President

Kennedy asked for the support of the American people. He said:

> My fellow citizens, let no one doubt that this is a difficult and dangerous effort on which we have set out. No one can foresee precisely what course it will take, or what costs or casualties will be incurred . . . But the greatest danger of all would be to do nothing . . . One path we shall never choose, and that is the path of surrender or submission . . .

In the days that followed, President Kennedy received a tremendous outpouring of support from all around the country. Many newspapers, television commentators, and others supported the president's decision strongly and explained to people why it was necessary.

Of course, people were very frightened too. For the first time, there was a real danger of a nuclear war starting within a few days, *and people knew it.* At no time, before or since, have Americans been so afraid of a nuclear war.

THE CLIMAX OF THE CRISIS

During the crisis, the United States took many other actions, including preparing for war with the Soviet Union. This was only realistic. But Kennedy and his advisors mainly wanted to discourage the Soviets from wanting war at all.

An example of a step Kennedy took involves the B-52 bombers. Naturally, all the bombers were made ready to take off from their bases at short notice. Another step was taken too. President Kennedy ordered that some of the B-52s be moved to civilian airports around the country and kept there, ready to take off.

During the crisis there were B-52 bombers parked at many civilian airports that served American cities. The bombers were parked on the outer runways, as far from the passenger terminals as possible; but of course they were in plain view. The bombers had nuclear bombs aboard and were ready at all times to take off immediately.

This had never been done before, and many Americans found it frightening. Obviously, it meant that the United States was really getting ready to fight a nuclear war.

But President Kennedy had a good reason for parking the B-52s at the airports. If the B-52s were scattered, the Soviets could not destroy all of them. The Soviets did not have enough ICBMs to attack all the bases *and* all the airports where B-52s were parked. Even if the Soviets launched all their ICBMs, many B-52s would survive. Those B-52s could then strike back at the U.S.S.R.

This is another example of how the strange logic of deterrence works. President Kennedy ordered something that many people found frightening, but his action actually made the situation safer and a nuclear war *less* likely. He made sure the Soviet leaders would not imagine they could destroy America's ability for **retaliation.**

THE RESOLUTION OF THE CRISIS

At the same time that he was taking steps to prepare for war, President Kennedy also tried to reassure the

Soviets. He sent messages to Moscow, making it clear that the United States did not want a war. He said repeatedly that American military preparations were only a precaution. All that the U.S. demanded was that the Soviet missiles be removed from Cuba and no more sent.

After days of anxious waiting, the Soviets agreed. Some ships on their way to Cuba turned around in the middle of the ocean and headed back to the U.S.S.R. On Sunday, October 28, 1962, the U.S. received official confirmation from Moscow that the Soviet government accepted Kennedy's terms. The Soviet troops in Cuba began dismantling the missiles there, and these too were shipped back to the U.S.S.R.

President Kennedy had won. The crisis was over. There was no nuclear war.

WHY?

For many years afterward, American experts debated why the Soviets had done something so rash. Why had they run the terrible risk of war?

Of course one reason was that they hoped that the U.S. would not find out what was occurring until too late. They put the missiles into Cuba secretly, hoping the missiles could be made ready before the U.S. discovered them.

But the Soviets must have realized that there was a good chance that the United States would find out before the missiles were ready. Why did they run that risk?

Experts think that one reason may have been that the Soviets thought President Kennedy was young and inexperienced. They may have thought he would simply back down.

There are other possible reasons, too. One important reason involves the arms race.

In the late 1950s, many American experts had worried that there would be a missile gap in the period 1960–62. But in fact there was no missile gap. The Soviets did not deploy many ICBMs. By the middle of 1962, there were fewer than seventy-five Soviet ICBMs deployed.

No one in Washington understood at the time why there were so few. Later it was learned that the earliest Soviet ICBMs did not work very well. The Soviets had run into technical difficulties. So they decided to deploy only a few of them. Meantime, work was being completed on the American ICBMs. These missiles did work, and the U.S. began developing them as rapidly as possible.

This is another example of the arms race. American officials expected the Soviets to deploy many ICBMs. Each month, they expected that *now* the Soviets would deploy many. So they felt it was urgent that the U.S. deploy as many as possible, as soon as possible.

A MISSILE GAP IN REVERSE

The result was that a missile gap did develop in the early 1960s, but instead of the U.S. being behind the Soviets as everyone expected, the Soviets ended up being behind the U.S. By 1962, there was a missile gap in reverse.

In October of 1962, when the Cuban Missile Crisis occurred, the Soviet Union had about 75 ICBMs, and the United States had about 225. The U.S. was also deploying more, very fast. (For instance, only eight months later the U.S. had more than five hundred.)

Now you can see another possible reason why the Soviets decided to risk putting missiles in Cuba. They had a great many short-range missiles available. Short-range missiles could not reach the U.S. if they were launched from the Soviet Union, but they could easily reach the U.S. if they were launched from Cuba. Many experts came to the conclusion that the Soviets put short-range missiles into Cuba to try to change the balance instantly.

THE PROBLEM OF A FIRST STRIKE

In fact, the Soviets could have put so many missiles into Cuba that some people throught they might have eventually gained a first-strike capability. (You recall that a first-strike capability is the ability to disarm the other country by striking first.) Ironically, the United States probably *did* have, or was close to having, a first-strike capability at this time!

By October of 1962 the U.S. had so many ICBMs and the Soviet Union had so few that the Soviets must have been worried. Furthermore, officials in Washington had revealed that they knew the *exact* location of every Soviet ICBM and every Soviet bomber base.

In Moscow, it must have seemed that the United States was gaining a first-strike capability. Of course, the Soviets had no reason to think the U.S. would use this advantage to actually begin a war. The U.S. hadn't begun a war even when it had a nuclear monopoly in the late 1940s. Even so, an American first-strike capability probably made the Soviets nervous. Some U.S. experts later concluded that this may have been one of the Soviets' reasons for putting missiles in Cuba.

SUMMARY

The greatest crisis between the U.S. and the Soviet Union occurred in October of 1962. It is called the "Cuban Missile Crisis." (See Figure 14.) The Soviets secretly put nuclear missiles in Cuba, while saying repeatedly that they never would. They hoped the United States would not uncover the lie before the missiles were ready for launch; at that point the U.S. would not be able to do anything.

But the U.S. found out about the missiles in time. President Kennedy decided to reject the first choice his advisors suggested—an immediate air attack on the missiles in Cuba. Instead he tried a public demand for their removal and a naval blockade of Cuba to prevent any more missiles from arriving. He knew

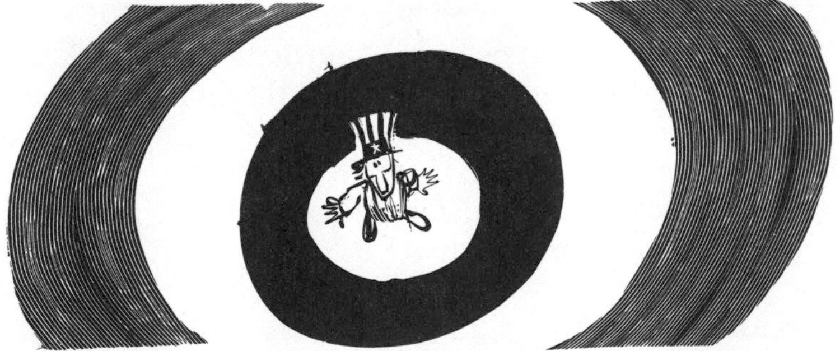

***Figure 14** Soviet missiles in Cuba would have made the U.S. far more vulnerable to attack.*

he could still order the air attack if his first effort failed.

After an extremely tense few days, during which the U.S. prepared for war if necessary, the Soviets backed down and agreed to Kennedy's demands. The Cuban Missile Crisis was over.

Why did the Soviets try something so rash? We may never know all the reasons. Probably one reason is that they were trying to catch up in the arms race. Short-range missiles in Cuba could make up for the "missile gap in reverse"—the huge American lead in ICBMs.

REVIEW QUESTIONS

1. What was the name of the leader of Cuba during the Cuban Missile Crisis, and when did he come to power?
2. President Kennedy said that no one would be killed if the plan he announced on television worked. Why?
3. Why did the president order some of the B-52 bombers to be parked at regular civilian airports?
4. Why did the Soviets decide to deploy very few ICBMs in 1960, 1961, and 1962?
5. How many ICBMs did each side have at the time of the Cuban Missile Crisis?
6. Give some reasons why Soviet leaders may have been worried in 1962 about a U.S. first-strike capability.

PERSONALITY PROFILE

John F. Kennedy

John F. Kennedy, thirty-fifth president of the United States, was born on May 29, 1917. At age 43, he was the United States' youngest president; he was also the first Roman Catholic president.

Jack Kennedy grew up in the Boston area and went to college at Harvard. As a senior there, he wrote a long paper on why Great Britain was so slow in building up its armed forces in the face of rapid armament by Nazi Germany. After graduating he published it as a book, called *Why England Slept*. His timing was perfect; the book appeared just after France fell to the Nazis. The book became a best seller in both England and America.

Kennedy served as a naval officer in the Pacific during World War II, and was decorated for his heroism. (His adventures were later made into a movie, *P.T. 109*.)

After the war Kennedy ran for a seat in the U.S. house of Representatives and won it, although he was only twenty-nine. In 1952 he ran for and won a seat in the U.S. Senate.

Hospitalized for a long period in 1954 for back troubles (caused partly by his war injuries), he wrote a second book. This one was about American leaders who had done what they believed was right even when it was unpopular. Called *Profiles in Courage,* the book won a Pulitzer Prize.

Kennedy ran for president against Richard Nixon in 1960 and won by a very thin margin—about 120 thousand votes, out of seventy million votes cast. (This is less than ¼ of one percent.) In his inaugural address, he offered Americans a famous slogan: "Ask not what your country can do for you; ask what you can do for your country." As president, Kennedy created the first government agency devoted to controlling the arms race, the Arms Control and Disarmament Agency (ACDA), which still exists.

President Kennedy was assassinated on November 22, 1963.

5 Stable Deterrence

What are "secure" weapons?
What is an SLBM?
What does "parity" mean?
What is "stable deterrence" and why is it important?

In the years following the Cuban Missile Crisis, the arms race did not end, but it developed in a way that made the United States and the Soviet Union more equal. This equality was not deliberate. Each country wanted to achieve superiority, but neither was able to.

THE NEXT GENERATION

American scientists were not satisfied with the first kinds of ICBMs that they built, and they promptly began work on a more advanced ICBM. This kind of progression from a less advanced to a more advanced weapon happens constantly in the arms race. Experts call it moving to "the next generation."

In the early 1960s, the United States quickly moved to the next generation of ICBMs. Most of the first-generation ICBMs were removed. President Kennedy decided that the United States would deploy one thousand of the second-generation ICBMs. In addition, fifty-four of the best first-generation ICBMs were kept. For many years thereafter, the United States kept 1,054 ICBMs deployed.

The Soviets also moved quickly to their own second-generation ICBMs. These ICBMs worked better than earlier Soviet missiles. Now the Soviets could deploy many ICBMs. By the middle of the 1960s, the buildup of Soviet ICBMs that American experts had long been expecting finally began. The Soviets deployed missiles rapidly, just as the U.S. already had. This ended the "missile gap in reverse." The Soviets rapidly caught up. By the end of the 1960s they had deployed as many ICBMs as the U.S. had.

SECURE ICBMs

Both the U.S.S.R. and the U.S. also put their ICBMs underground during the 1960s, to protect their missiles in the event of an attack. To do this, American and Soviet scientists developed long steel cylinders for storing the ICBMs. These cylinders are called "silos," because they look like the grain silos found on farms. Each ICBM silo is placed in the ground vertically, with a heavy steel door on top. (See Figure 16.) Underground in a silo with the steel door closed, an ICBM is well protected. A nuclear warhead could explode fairly close by, and the missile would not be damaged. If a missile were launched, the steel door would open and the missile would be fired right out of the silo.

Naturally a direct hit with a nuclear blast would destroy the silo and the missile. But in the 1960s

Figure 16 This photo shows an ICBM in an underground silo.

neither the U.S.S.R. nor the U.S. could fire missiles across the globe accurately enough to score direct hits. Therefore, ICBMs were safe from attack. As experts put it, they were **secure weapons.** By the end of the 1960s, each country had more than a thousand "secure" ICBMs.

SLBMs

Meanwhile, another kind of missile was developed by both the United States and the U.S.S.R. Scientists had been thinking about putting missiles out at sea. They realized, however, that the missiles wouldn't be secure on ships that cruise around on the surface. Ships on the surface are easy to spot, and once spotted they are easy to sink.

Scientists realized that missiles put in submarines, which cruise under the sea, would be hard to find. It would be better still if the submarine didn't have to surface to fire its missiles but could fire while remaining submerged.

Exactly this system was developed, first by the United States and then by the Soviet Union. The U.S. had this kind of missile-carrying submarine at sea by the early 1960s. The Soviets had it by the late 1960s.

A missile that is carried by a submarine and can be fired from below the surface is called a *Submarine-Launched Ballistic Missile,* or **SLBM** for short.

Most experts believe that SLBMs are especially valuable for maintaining deterrence. Deterrence requires that each country be sure that the other country can and will retaliate, no matter what. Since SLBMs are practically impossible to locate, the SLBMs cannot be destroyed. These secure SLBMs assure that either country *could* retaliate even after being attacked. This is one main reason why both countries deployed the SLBMs, even though both already had ICBMs and bombers. (See Figure 17.)

PARITY

In the 1960s the United States built more than six hundred SLBMs and forty-one submarines to carry them. By the end of the decade, the U.S.S.R. had equalled these numbers. By 1969 the U.S. and the Soviet Union were roughly equal in their ICBMs and SLBMs. Though a few years earlier the U.S. was

Figure 17 This photo shows the submarine USS **Georgia**, *one of the U.S. subs carrying SLBMs.*

ahead in both categories, the Soviet Union gained approximate equality with the U.S. in missile forces within a few years.

Nuclear weapons are so enormously destructive that it does not matter if one side has *slightly* more or *slightly* fewer than the other side. What does matter is a state of approximate equality (or great inequality). This state of rough equality is called **parity.**

Parity in missile forces never existed before 1969. The fact that the Soviet Union had achieved parity was very important. It gave the U.S.S.R. an appearance of equal military standing with the U.S. By 1970 something else had happened that was even more important than parity in missiles. That is something so important that, in a basic way, it has controlled everything that has happened since.

SECURE FORCES AND DETERRENCE

You recall that at the time when American experts had feared the missile gap, they had been afraid that the Soviets might be able to destroy all the U.S. B-52 bomber bases at one blow. During the Cuban Missile Crisis, President Kennedy had thought about the same possibility. The B-52 bases were vulnerable. President Kennedy had taken the precaution of scattering the B-52s so that the Soviets would not be tempted to destroy them all at once. In other words, the experts and the president had worried about the Soviets having a first-strike capability.

Perhaps the Soviets also worried at times about the United States having a first-strike capability. In the early 1960s the U.S. was deploying ICBMs rapidly, and the U.S.S.R. had only a few.

But by the end of the 1960s, the situation was totally different. Both countries had placed their ICBMs in underground silos, where they were secure. Both countries had many SLBMs, which were also secure because the submarines carrying them could not be located.

So by the end of the 1960s, the missiles on both sides were secure. Only the bomber bases were vulnerable. The bomber bases became less important, however, because by now the countries had over a thousand secure ICBMs and hundreds of secure SLBMs. In short, by now *most of both sides' forces were secure.*

This development was of fundamental importance.

This was more important than parity in numbers because this is the ideal situation for mutual deterrence. Mutual deterrence, you recall, means that each country knows that the other can and will retaliate if attacked. Each country knows the other can absorb an attack and still have adequate forces left to strike back.

If both countries know this, then each will surely be deterred from attacking in the first place. Obviously, if neither attacks, peace will be maintained. This is the basic idea and purpose of deterrence.

Hence, the ideal situation for mutual deterrence is for both sides to have adequate *secure* forces. This is precisely the situation that developed by the end of the 1960s.

STABLE DETERRENCE

Experts have a term for any situation in which a large percentage of *both* countries' nuclear weapons are secure. The term is **stable deterrence.**

Conversely, if a high percentage of *either* country's weapons are vulnerable, experts call the situation "unstable." An unstable situation is not necessarily one where a war will occur soon, but it *is* a situation where mutual deterrence is not as certain and not as reliable.

Stability or instability is a matter of degree. It is not clear-cut. As long as a considerable percentage of all weapons are secure, the situation is stable. Most experts feel that it will remain fairly stable even if the percentage of stable weapons drops below half. Exactly at what point the situation starts to become unstable is a matter of judgment. Experts disagree about where this point is. They do agree that it certainly is unstable if nearly all the weapons of either country are vulnerable.

One country has a "first-strike capability" when the other country's weapons are vulnerable. This vulnerability practically "invites" attack because the first country may think it can strike and remain relatively unharmed. This is a general principle that applies at all times and under all circumstances. It applied to bomber bases in the 1950s, and it could apply to weapons in outer space in the future. Vulnerable weapons may practically invite attack, whereas secure weapons help make deterrence stable.

ANOTHER NAME FOR THE SAME THING

There is another phrase for stable deterrence. That phrase is "Mutual Assured Destruction," often abbreviated **MAD.** This is a frightening phrase. It sounds awful. Nobody finds it attractive or likeable. But its basic meaning is the same.

You may remember from Chapter Two that another term for deterrence is an "assured destruction capability." If one country has an assured destruction capability against the other, that means that the stronger country is sure that it can penetrate the other's defenses and destroy the other's cities. A *mutual* assured destruction capability simply means that both countries feel they can destroy the other. If both countries continue to be sure of this all the time, this is also stable deterrence. Neither country will attack because both know that both will be destroyed no matter who strikes first.

SUMMARY

The important development of the 1960s was that the world moved from a dangerously unstable situation to a much more stable one.

You now understand why. At the time of the missile gap fears, and again during the Cuban Missile Crisis, American experts were worried that U.S. nuclear forces were vulnerable. The Soviets may have worried about their forces being vulnerable, too. (It is perfectly possible for both countries' forces to be vulnerable at the same time. That would be the most dangerous situation of all.) Many experts think that the Cuban Missile Crisis was a "symptom" of this basic situation; deterrence between the two countries was unstable.

Deterrence became stable by the end of the 1960s. Since then there have been hardly any U.S.-Soviet crises and none like the Cuban Missile Crisis. Most experts feel that we have been living in a safer world ever since.

Of course, most people feel the world is not nearly safe *enough* yet. That is what much of the rest of this book will be about. But it has been a safer world since deterrence was made stable.

REVIEW QUESTIONS

1. In the context of weapons, what does a "generation" mean?
2. What is an ICBM "silo"?
3. Name one "secure" missile system and tell why it is secure.

4. Why was it important that the U.S.S.R. achieved parity with the United States in nuclear weapons?
5. By the late 1960s, most strategic weapons on both sides were secure. What did this mean for deterrence?
6. What does "Mutual Assured Destruction" mean?

6 Arms Control

What does "arms control" mean?
What were the early arms control agreements?
What does SALT mean, and why is it important?
What is an ABM, and why was an ABM Treaty needed?

After the Baruch Plan failed in the late 1940s, the U.S. and U.S.S.R. did not try any further negotiations on nuclear weapons for a while. In the mid-1950s they resumed talking. Before long, they concluded they would not be able to get rid of nuclear weapons entirely. They could make no progress discussing complete *disarmament*.

Experts then came up with a new approach called **arms control.** Under this approach, the U.S. and U.S.S.R. would try to get the arms race under control. They would try to slow the arms race down, then halt it. If they succeeded in this much, they could later turn to actually getting rid of weapons.

In 1961, for instance, the U.S. secretary of state, Dean Rusk, had this to say in testimony before Congress:

> [We must pursue] the hope of achieving some

> measure of control over the ever-expanding upward spiral of armaments. . . . Our own basic policies require that we make strong, patient, and sincere efforts to do everything possible to create conditions under which nations can safely reduce their armaments, and thereby alleviate the dangers inherent in an uncontrolled arms race.

This step-by-step approach seemed more feasible than trying to accomplish complete disarmament all at once. Because it would occur gradually, arms control seemed like something that might succeed. But even with this more modest approach, it was years before the U.S. and the U.S.S.R. were able to come to any agreement.

EARLY AGREEMENTS REACHED

The Cuban Missile Crisis had frightened officials in both Washington and Moscow. It showed that nuclear war was a real possibility. The fear created by the Crisis caused both countries to want to control the arms race more than ever before.

After the Cuban Missile Crisis, two arms control agreements were reached quickly. They were useful beginnings, although neither one applied to the most important part of the arms race—the race for new weapons and more weapons.

The U.S.S.R. and the U.S. agreed to create the Hot Line. The Hot Line would allow for high-speed communication between the president in Washington and the general secretary in Moscow. High-speed communication between them had not existed before.

Because of the way the Hot Line has been portrayed

in popular films, many people think that the Hot Line is two red telephones—one on the president's desk in Washington and one on the general secretary's desk in Moscow. Actually, the Hot Line is two fast teletype machines—one in the White House basement and the other in a similar place in Moscow. Experts decided that a fast teletype would be better than a telephone. A conversation over a telephone line could be misunderstood. In an intense crisis like the Cuban Missile Crisis a misunderstanding could be fatal. Experts felt that printed messages transmitted between the two leaders would be less likely to lead to misunderstanding.

The U.S. and U.S.S.R. also agreed to stop testing nuclear weapons above ground or at sea. The Limited Test Ban Treaty, as it was called, was signed while Kennedy was president, and the treaty came into force only weeks before he was assassinated. Before this treaty, both countries had often tested in the open air. This testing was creating radioactive **fallout**. In a nuclear explosion, very fine dust is sucked up into the upper atmosphere, and it is made radioactive. It then falls out of the atmosphere over a span of weeks, months, or even years. These radioactive particles endanger peoples' health all over the world. By ending all tests above ground, the U.S. and the U.S.S.R. halted the creation of fallout. Within a few years there was almost none.

However, the Limited Test Ban Treaty allowed both countries to continue to test nuclear weapons underground. An underground test does not cause dust to be lifted into the atmosphere. Permitting underground tests, though, meant that the development of new weapons would continue.

STABLE DETERRENCE AND ARMS CONTROL

Why weren't the two countries able to agree on more than these two points? Most experts think that one main reason was that deterrence was still unstable at this time. Both countries were trying to gain superiority.

The United States was first to have superiority in the 1940s and 1950s. When *Sputnik* was launched in 1957, however, it looked as though the U.S.S.R. would gain superiority. *Sputnik* meant the U.S.S.R. would soon have ICBMs. Actually, it turned out that the U.S. was the first to deploy ICBMs in quantity because the earliest Soviet ICBMs didn't work very well. Then, in 1962 the Soviets tried to turn the tables by secretly sending missiles to Cuba. In short, superiority had passed back and forth throughout this time.

But during the 1960s, the situation moved toward stable deterrence. Each country put its ICBMs underground and built SLBMs. By the late 1960s each country had many *secure* weapons, and the U.S. and U.S.S.R. were in parity.

Most experts think that these are the chief reason that the two countries felt able at this point to talk about real limits on the arms race. Deterrrence had to be stable, and the two countries had to be roughly in parity. Then, and only then, could the U.S. and the U.S.S.R. talk about stopping their attempts to gain superiority.

SALT

In the late 1960s, American officials proposed to the Soviets that the two countries discuss putting limits on the arms race. After some delay, the Soviets agreed. Talks between the two countries began in 1969 and were called the *Strategic Arms Limitation Talks,* or **SALT** for short. (In reference to nuclear weapons, the word **strategic** refers to Soviet ICBMs, SLBMs, and bombers that can attack the United States; or to American ICBMs, SLBMs, and bombers that can attack the U.S.S.R. Naturally, strategic weapons are the ones each side considers most important.)

There are many other kinds of nuclear weapons, but those were excluded from SALT. The U.S. and the U.S.S.R. wanted to concentrate on the strategic weapons first and discuss other problems later.

It took until 1972 for the two countries to reach some agreements. Those agreements are called the "SALT I Agreements." (See Figure 18.)(Later there were SALT II Agreements.) The SALT I Agreements

***Figure 18** President Nixon and General Secretary Brezhnev signing the SALT I Agreements in Moscow in 1972.*

were formally signed on May 26, 1972. The U.S. president, Richard Nixon, went to Moscow to sign them. He and the Soviet general secretary, Leonid Brezhnev, signed the Agreements at a ceremony in the Kremlin. (See Figure 18.)

The SALT I Agreements were divided into two parts. One part was an agreement that limited the *maximum number* of ICBMs and SLBMs that the U.S. and the U.S.S.R. could build. In other words, a "ceiling" was put on the number of missiles each country could have.

This agreement allowed the U.S.S.R. somewhat more missiles than it allowed the United States. Small differences, however, don't matter much as long as deterrence is stable. The agreement also made up for the difference by allowing the United States some other advantages. The specific terms of this agreement are shown in Table I.

This agreement was originally supposed to last for five years. Both the United States and the U.S.S.R., however, said later that they would continue to abide by the terms of the agreement, and they still do today.

ABMs AND THE ABM TREATY

To understand the other part of the SALT I Agreements, you need to learn about another complication that had developed in the arms race. During the 1960s, scientists in both the United States and the U.S.S.R. had continued to think about the problem of a defense against ICBMs or SLBMs. They decided, as they had earlier, that an adequate missile defense system was impossible. ICBM and SLBM warheads

Table I

The SALT I Agreement on limiting ICBMs and SLBMs

	U.S.	U.S.S.R.
ICBMs	1,054	1,618
SLBMs	710	950
Submarines for carrying SLBMs	44	62

The Soviet advantage in numbers was made up for in three ways. First, the agreement did not cover bombers, in which the U.S. had a large advantage.

Second, at this time the American ICBMs, SLBMs, and submarines were technically superior to the Soviet ones. For instance, the American missiles were more accurate, more reliable, and could be launched more quickly.

Third, the agreements did not cover a large number of U.S. shorter-range missiles and bombers that were located in Europe and Asia, and which could be used to attack the U.S.S.R. The Soviets had nothing comparable. (American nuclear weapons had been in Europe and Asia for a long time and had been deployed there openly and legally.)

were too small and moved too fast to be intercepted and destroyed.

But scientists decided that while no system could destroy *all* incoming warheads, it might be possible to destroy *some*. Scientists developed another kind of missile to do this. A missile intended to intercept and destroy an ICBM or SLBM was called an *Anti-Ballistic Missile*, or an **ABM** for short.

This development posed a new problem for the experts who were trying to control the arms race. If one side built ABMs to shoot down some incoming missiles, the other side would surely build more ICBMs or SLBMs to attack with.

This kind of situation had actually happened in the 1950s when the U.S.S.R. developed an air defense system and the United States built more B-52s to be sure of penetrating the Soviet system. Experts feared that the same thing would happen now with missiles. If the Soviets deployed ABMs, the United States would deploy more ICBMs and SLBMs to be sure of penetrating the Soviet ABMs. Or if the United States deployed ABMs, the U.S.S.R. would deploy more ICBMs and SLBMs to be sure of penetrating the American ABMs.

Building more and more ICBMs and SLBMs would accelerate the arms race, yet many experts were trying to halt the arms race. Stopping the buildup of ICBMs and SLBMs was the whole point of SALT. How could this problem be solved?

There was only one solution. Neither side could be allowed to *have* ABMs. (Or they could have only very few.) This is why the SALT I Agreements had to have two parts. One part put a numerical ceiling on ICBMs and SLBMs. The other part was a treaty to make sure those ceilings would hold.

A formal treaty is a more serious document and represents a stronger commitment than other agreements. So the ABM Treaty had to be submitted for **ratification** (legal approval) by the U. S. Senate. It was ratified by a vote of eighty-eight to two. This treaty has no time limit, so it will continue in force indefinitely.

The ABM Treaty stated that neither country would build more than a tiny number of ABMs. In 1972 the number was set at 200; two years later it was reduced to 100. Obviously, such small numbers of ABMs could never shoot down the large number of ICBMs and SLBMs that each side had.

REACTION TO THE SALT I AGREEMENTS

Many people were pleased when the SALT I Agreements were signed. It meant that some kind of limits were being put on the arms race. The agreements did not yet cover everything, but a beginning had been made.

During the late 1960s and early 1970s, the U.S. and Soviet Union also reached several other, less important, arms control agreements. The SALT I Agreements, in conjunction with these others, gave people the feeling that real progress was being made. Many people hoped that the U.S. and the U.S.S.R. would quickly reach further agreements that would halt the arms race more completely. Those hopes were dashed. There wasn't another important agreement for seven years, and that agreement didn't control much. The next chapter explains why.

SUMMARY

Because it proved too difficult to discuss complete disarmament, the U.S. and the U.S.S.R. decided in the 1960s to work instead on *arms control*—the slowing down and halting of the arms race. Partly because both countries were frightened by the Cuban Missile Crisis, they reached two agreements quickly: the Hot Line and the Limited Test Ban Treaty, which ended nuclear fallout.

Next the two countries turned to the arms race itself and opened the Strategic Arms Limitation Talks (SALT). The SALT I Agreements of 1972 consisted of two parts. One part established ceilings for each country's ICBMs and SLBMs. The other part was a permanent treaty that banned Anti-Ballistic Missiles (ABMs) beyond a token number. The U.S. Senate approved the ABM Treaty by a vote of eighty-eight to two.

REVIEW QUESTIONS

1. Why is the Hot Line a fast teletype system and not a telephone system?
2. What feature of the Limited Test Ban Treaty allowed testing of nuclear weapons to continue?
3. What happened during the 1960s that many experts believe allowed the two sides to reach an agreement limiting strategic weapons?
4. Which country originally proposed talks on limiting strategic weapons? What year did the talks begin?
5. When, where, and by whom were the SALT I Agreements signed?
6. Originally, how long were the ceilings on ICBMs and SLBMs supposed to last? Have they been extended?
7. Experts believed the ceilings on ICBMs and SLBMs would not hold for long unless both sides were prohibited from building many ABMs. Why?

7 New Technology

What is a MIRV?
What are the SALT II Agreements?
Why were there new fears of Soviet superiority?
What effect did the anti-nuclear war movement have?

The main reason that it took so long for the U.S. and the U.S.S.R. to reach any further agreement after SALT I was that scientists in both countries were developing new technology. The new technology made the arms race still more complicated.

As had happened many times before, new weapons were invented by American scientists first, but Soviet scientists were close behind.

MIRVs

Until about the time of SALT I, all missiles had carried only one warhead. Then scientists discovered a way to put multiple warheads on a single missile. With this new system, all the warheads were carried together until the missile rose above the atmosphere. Then the missile launched the warheads one by one.

Each of the warheads could be aimed at a *different* target. A single missile could destroy not just one target, but as many separate targets as it had warheads. (See Figure 19.)

Experts gave this new system for "delivering" warheads a name that is a real mouthful: *Multiple, Independently-targetable, Re-entry Vehicles.* For short, they are called **MIRVs** (pronounced to rhyme with "curves").

MIRVs were a valuable new weapon from a military point of view, which is why both the U.S. and the U.S.S.R. built them as soon as possible. MIRVs had

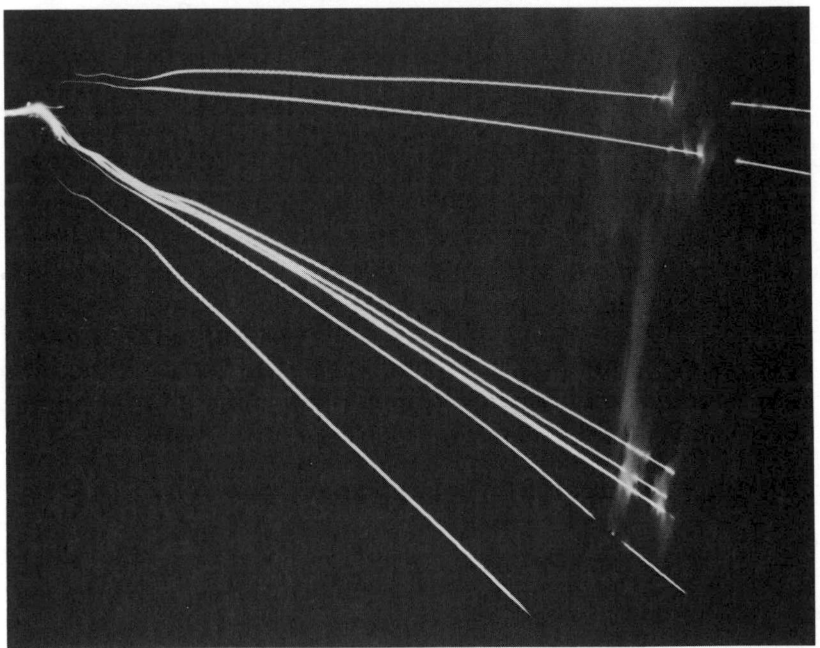

***Figure 19** This time-exposure photograph shows eight separate warheads from a single missile reentering the atmosphere during a flight test in the South Pacific in 1983.*

much more destructive power. For instance, American submarines could carry sixteen missiles. If they were missiles with single warheads, that meant sixteen warheads per submarine. But if they were the MIRVed missiles carrying ten warheads each, that added up to a total of 160 warheads per submarine.

You can see, however, that this also presented a big problem for arms control. Obviously, the invention of MIRVs would make it possible for both the U.S. and the U.S.S.R. to increase the total number of nuclear warheads. But arms control meant *stopping* the growth of destructive power on both sides.

For a while, arms control experts hoped that the two countries could agree to build very few missiles carrying MIRVs, or none at all. If they could agree on this, MIRVs would not become a serious problem.

But no agreement like this was reached. During the 1970s, American and Soviet officials argued about what sort of limits, if any, could be put on MIRVs. While they were arguing, both countries replaced their single-warhead missiles with MIRVed missiles as fast as they could.

The number of *warheads* each side could "deliver" grew rapidly, even though both sides stayed within the SALT I ceilings on *missiles*. By the end of the 1970s, the U.S. had about eight thousand nuclear warheads and the U.S.S.R. seven thousand. (Both sides continued to build more in the 1980s.)

SALT II

When the U.S. and U.S.S.R. signed the SALT I Agreements in 1972, they promised each other and the world that they would begin work right away on new agreements that would control the arms race more completely. The new agreements would be called SALT II.

At first it looked as though the SALT II Agreements might be reached by 1975, but the arguments over MIRVs (and other things) became too complex. Salt II dragged on and on.

Finally in 1979, the two countries were ready to sign the SALT II Agreements. This time the signing ceremony was held in Vienna. Again the U.S. president, this time Jimmy Carter, and Soviet General Secretary Leonid Brezhnev went there to sign the agreements. The signing ceremony was on the eighteenth of June.

PERSONALITY PROFILE

LEONID BREZHNEV

Leonid Brezhnev (Figure 20) was the main leader of the Soviet Union for eighteen years, from 1964 until his death in 1982. During the earlier part of that time he shared some of his power with other men, but gradually gathered more to himself as time passed. Because of his long period in office, he signed both the SALT I and SALT II Agreements, as well as several other arms control agreements. Brezhnev had always advocated military strength, and after he came to power the U.S.S.R. undertook a long, steady military buildup. But he also wanted good relations with the West and believed arms control was one way to achieve it.

The SALT II Agreements that the two men signed that day are extremely complicated. Even the most important elements are complicated, but a couple of major points will be mentioned here.

In dealing with the problem of MIRVs, the agreements created *sublimits,* as experts call them. The agreements kept the ceiling on missiles that SALT I had created; in fact, the new agreements slightly reduced the permitted number. Under that ceiling, the new agreements set, for example, a lower ceiling, or sublimit, on the number of MIRVed SLBMs each side could have.

Some experts felt that these sublimits were not too important. The numbers were set in such a way that neither the U.S. nor the U.S.S.R. had to give up any missiles they had already built or were planning to build. (The Soviets agreed to "give up" a few old missiles they were going to scrap anyway.) This was the only way the U.S. and U.S.S.R. could reach an agreement at all.

THE DEBATE OVER SALT II

Just as in 1972, one part—the more important part—of the SALT II Agreements was in the form of a treaty. President Carter submitted the treaty to the Senate. The Senate then debated whether it would ratify this treaty.

The debate was heated. Some senators were strongly in favor of the treaty; others were strongly against it. Because the treaty was so complicated, there was a lot of debate simply over what its implications *were*—as well as over how people felt about those implications.

The senators who favored the treaty felt that it did put *some* further limits on the arms race and that it was important to keep on making agreements, lest the two sides give up trying to control the arms race at all. For example, former Senator Gary Hart (Democrat of Colorado) said in a speech that "SALT agreements of this sort, however inadequate, largely or substantially enhance the chances against nuclear war. . . . Without continued advances in the areas of trying to limit strategic systems, then the lid is off."

The senators who opposed the treaty felt that it didn't control the expansion of Soviet weapons enough, and that it put too many controls on the development of U.S. weapons. For example, Senator Robert Byrd (Democrat of Virginia) said in a speech that he thought that the Soviets were ahead already and might soon achieve new technical breakthroughs. "Russia could seize the unilateral advantage obtained and deny to the United States a similar system. Under SALT II, Russia would have a sufficient advantage in strategic offensive systems to deny the American deployment of a new technology Russia achieved first. . . ."

Some senators were concerned about **verification.** At all times the U.S. must be able to "verify" that the Soviet Union is living up to the terms of any agreement. For SALT I, verification was not difficult because U.S. satellites orbiting in space can take very detailed photographs of Soviet territory. But people were not sure that everything included in SALT II could be photographed from space. For instance, what goes on inside buildings cannot be photographed. Senators debated whether or not satellite photography and other techniques would provide enough verification. The Senate debate continued through the autumn of 1979.

Then, in late December, the Soviet Union invaded Afghanistan. This invasion disturbed and angered people throughout America and the West. Because of the invasion, the Senate was not about to approve *any* new agreement with the Soviet Union! President Carter withdrew the treaty from consideration for the time being.

Ronald Reagan said often during his campaign for the presidency that he was opposed to the treaty. When Reagan became president in 1980, he announced that he would never resubmit it to the Senate.

PRESIDENT REAGAN AND SALT II

President Reagan also announced, however, that the United States would abide by the treaty so long as the U.S.S.R. did. Some people found this strange. Why should the U.S. abide by the treaty if the president disapproved of it and the Senate had not yet ratified it?

In 1986, President Reagan announced that the U.S. would cease to abide by the SALT II Treaty. He gave several reasons. One was that, when it was signed in 1979, the treaty had a time limit: It would expire at the end of 1985. Since the treaty was due to expire anyway, why should the U.S. respect it thereafter?

Many experts disagreed with the president's decision. They pointed out that the original SALT I ceilings also had a time limit, but both countries had kept renewing the SALT I ceilings. Why not do the same with this treaty?

CRUISE MISSILES

MIRVs were not the only new technology that made the problem of the arms race more complicated. Another new weapon, the **cruise missile,** was also invented.

A cruise missile is a small missile with wings. Unlike a ballistic missile, which goes up into space and then plunges down, a cruise missile flies horizontally, like an airplane. You can think of a cruise missile as a small robot aircraft. (See figure 21.)

A cruise missile is so small that it can be carried by a large airplane, transported on land by a truck or a

Figure 21 This American cruise missile flies horizontally and can carry a nuclear warhead for more than one thousand miles.

tractor, or carried by a ship or a submarine at sea. In spite of its small size, a cruise missile can carry a nuclear warhead more than one thousand miles.

Because cruise missiles are not very expensive, both the U.S. and the U.S.S.R. can afford to build a great many of them. In the 1980s, both countries are building hundreds of them. Experts think that both countries may have thousands eventually.

The invention of cruise missiles made the arms race still more difficult to bring under control. The fact that they are so small and can be carried by so many kinds of vehicles created a real problem for those trying to control the arms race. Officials in Washington were not sure that U.S. intelligence agencies could determine just how many cruise missiles the U.S.S.R. had. Soviet officials felt the same uncertainty about their ability to find out how many cruise missiles the U.S. had.

Because of these complications, American and Soviet officials weren't able to reach agreement on how to control cruise missiles. The SALT II Agreements included almost no controls on them.

NEW FEARS OF THE SOVIET UNION

During the 1970s many Americans came to fear the Soviet Union more than they had a few years earlier. There were two main reasons.

One reason was that in the 1970s several small countries in Africa and Asia (Ethiopia, South Yemen, Mozambique, and Vietnam) joined the U.S.S.R. as new allies. Then, in December 1979 the Soviets invaded Afghanistan. Many Americans feared that Soviet power in the world was growing and that the Soviets were becoming more aggressive.

Of course, the United States is *also* constantly trying to gain new allies in Africa and Asia. And by now, most Soviet leaders have decided that their invasion of Afghanistan was a mistake.

But at the end of the 1970s, it looked to many Americans as if the Soviets were "on the march."

A "WINDOW OF VULNERABILITY?"

The other reason that fear of the U.S.S.R. grew involved the missiles you have now learned about. Some—not all—experts believed a new threat had arisen.

Over the years, both sides gradually improved the *accuracy* of their missiles. Back in the 1960s, an ICBM warhead might miss its target (in a test) by a half mile. But by the end of the 1970s, it might miss by only one-tenth of a mile.

You remember that the 1970s was also the time that both sides put MIRVs on their missiles. That meant that the Soviets had a great many more warheads than they had had earlier.

What some experts worried about was this: Perhaps the underground silos in which the U. S. kept its ICBMs were becoming vulnerable.

With the better accuracy and larger number of warheads the Soviets had, Soviets might feel that they could destroy nearly all the U.S. silos. The U. S., you recall, had only slightly more than one thousand silos. By 1980 the U.S.S.R. was approaching six thousand warheads on its ICBMs. If the Soviets attacked they could aim six warheads at *each* silo. Many experts thought they would have a good chance of destroying nearly every silo.

There were various things the United States could do about this, but it would be some years before these things could be done. In the meantime, the U.S. silos would be vulnerable.

The experts who worried about this danger called it the **window of vulnerability.** (It was a "window" because the U. S. could "close" it after a few years.)

Many other experts did not think this was a real danger. One reason, as you have learned, is that deterrence now was *stable*. The United States still had a large number of secure weapons—the SLBMs. But the experts who were worried didn't think that deterrence was stable *enough*. The argument about "the window of vulnerability" raged among the experts for years.

Other experts doubted that Soviet leaders could ever accept all the uncertainties involved in a massive nuclear strike. For instance, Henry Kissinger said this in a speech in 1976:

> Initiation of an all-out surprise attack would depend on substantial confidence that thousands of reentry vehicles launched in carefully coordinated attacks—from land, sea and air—would knock out all their targets thousands of miles away, with a timing and reliability exactly as predicted, before the other side launches any forces to preempt or retailaite. . . . Any miscalculation or technical failure would mean national catastrophe. Assertions that one side is 'ahead' by the margins now under discussion pale in significance when an attack would depend on decisions based on such massive uncertainties and risks.

PERSONALITY PROFILE

Henry A. Kissinger

Henry A. Kissinger is one of the most colorful men to have helped direct American foreign policy in this century. He also has been one of the most powerful, not counting presidents.

Born in Germany in 1923, he came with his parents to America at age fifteen. He served in the U. S. Army during World War II. After the war he went to Harvard, both for college and for his doctoral degree, and then stayed on for many years as a teacher.

During the late 1950s and 1960s, he worked closely with Nelson Rockefeller, ex-governor of New York State and a man whom many people expected to be president someday. Kissinger also wrote a series of books that made him famous among experts on foreign policy and the problems of nuclear weapons.

When Richard Nixon was elected president in 1968, he invited Kissinger to become his main advisor on national security. Kissinger accepted and rapidly became the second most powerful man in Washington. By his brilliance and by the force of his personality (plus Nixon's respect and trust), Kissinger came to dominate the government bureacracies in a way that few men have in recent decades.

After Nixon was reelected in 1972, he made Kissinger secretary of state (with the Senate's approval). When the great Watergate scandal brought Nixon's downfall, his successor, Gerald Ford, asked Kissinger to stay on as secretary of state. So Kissinger largely controlled American foreign policy for a full eight years, under two presidents.

Since then, Kissinger has maintained his world fame through further writings, through public speeches, and by offering commentaries from time to time on television.

PRESIDENT REAGAN'S VIEW

In the presidential campaign of 1980, Ronald Reagan spoke often about the danger to the world posed by the Soviet Union. He said he was worried about Soviet power and Soviet aggressiveness. He said there *was* a "window of vulnerability." After he became president, he took various steps to increase the number and power of American nuclear weapons.

President Reagan also put together a group of leading experts to study the "window of vulnerability" problem again. That commission decided there really was no "window of vulnerability," but it praised many of the steps that President Reagen had taken.

You recall that President Reagan was opposed to SALT II. He said, too, that any new arms control agreements should wait until after the United States had increased it nuclear strength. For the time being, therefore, he did not open any new talks with the Soviets about controlling nuclear weapons.

THE ANTI-NUCLEAR WAR MOVEMENT

In the early 1980s a great many Americans became worried about nuclear weapons, and the danger of there being a nuclear war someday. People noticed that the number of weapons kept growing and growing. And they started thinking about what a nuclear war would mean if it ever occurred.

Especially in 1982 and 1983, there was a strong political movement in America which focused on the nuclear arms race. It called itself the "peace movement," or the "anti-nuclear war movement." Many meetings were held all around the country to discuss the arms race and the nuclear danger. On June 12, 1982, there was a huge march in New York City. More than three-quarters of a million people marched, making this the largest single demonstration in all of American history. There were many other events, large and small, as well.

There was also a made-for-television movie called *The Day After*. ABC showed it nationwide on Sunday evening, November 20, 1983. The movie tried to show, in a dramatic way, that a nuclear war would mean the nearly total destruction of America. It estimated that more than 20 million Americans watched it that night. (See Figure 23.)

A FREEZE?

The anti-nuclear-war movement came up with a specific proposal for something to do. The proposal was called the *Freeze*.

By this time, people were getting impatient with arms control agreements so complicated that hardly anyone could understand them. The Freeze was intended to be an idea so simple that everyone could understand it and so obvious that everyone would support it.

The Freeze idea was to stop the arms race completely, right where it was. Both sides would "freeze"

Figure 23 A military band plays as the battleship USS **Missouri** *arrives in port during a cruise around the world. Protestors display signs of opposition in the background. The most widely supported public movement was the Freeze.*

all their plans and their deployments, just where they were. Neither side would build any more nuclear weapons, any more missiles, or any more bombers. Neither side would carry out any more underground nuclear tests. Both sides would simply keep what they had now. Once the Freeze was accomplished, the U.S.S.R. and the U.S. could begin discussing reducing the number of weapons. Many Americans liked this idea. Polls showed that two thirds to three fourths of the people supported it.

Two senators who advocated the Freeze, Ted Kennedy of Massachusetts and Mark Hatfield of Oregon, made this argument for it:

> The freeze would not be unfair to either side, be-

> cause both the U.S. and the Soviet Union are effectively equivalent in strategic nuclear power. . . . We are ahead in some areas, and they are ahead in others. But the present strategic balance gives us the best opportunity we may ever have to call a halt to and end the nuclear arms race.

However, President Reagan was opposed to the Freeze. And many experts agreed with him, although sometimes for reasons different from his. President Reagan (and some experts) said that at present the U.S. was behind in the arms race. So to freeze everything right at that point would simply lock the U.S. into an inferior position.

For instance, in March 1986 President Reagan said during a nationally televised news conference that "on balance the Soviet Union does have a definite margin of superiority—enough so there is risk. . . ." He remarked that a freeze would not only leave the Soviets with their advantage, but would also give them no reason to negotiate reductions. "If they're out ahead," he said, "and we're behind and we're asking them to cut down, and join us in getting down to a lower level, there isn't much incentive."

Many other experts said that the U.S. and the U.S.S.R. were in roughly an equal position overall. But they said the Freeze was an idea that looked simple, but would actually be complicted to carry out in practice.

Controversy and disagreement made it difficult for the Freeze to attract solid, lasting support. Gradually, the idea has faded away.

However, the anti-nuclear war movement did succeed in gaining enough political influence that President Reagan felt compelled to reopen talks with the U.S.S.R. So, after a period of no talks, the two sides sat down together again.

SUMMARY

New technology, especially MIRVs and cruise missiles, made it harder to reach a second SALT agreement than people had originally anticipated. SALT II was signed in 1979. But it was very complicated and aroused great controversy in the U.S. Senate. After the Soviets invaded Afghanistan, SALT II was withdrawn from Senate consideration. Although SALT II was never ratified, both the U.S. and the U.S.S.R. said they would abide by it. In 1985 President Reagan announced that the U.S. would no longer honor the agreement.

The late 1970s and early 1980s marked a time when many Americans feared the U.S.S.R. more than they had earlier. Several nations in Asia and Africa became Soviet allies, and the U.S.S.R. demonstrated in Afghanistan that it was willing to use military force. Some experts also worried that a "window of vulnerability" for American ICBMs was developing.

On the other hand, 1982 and 1983 saw a large "peace movement" in America, made up of people who were concerned about the possibility of nuclear war. A total "freeze" on the arms race was proposed, and while this was never adopted, citizen concern helped spur renewed talks.

REVIEW QUESTIONS

1. Give an example of how adding MIRVs multiplied the power of a missile-carrying submarine.

2. Explain how adding MIRVs allowed both sides to expand their destructive power while staying within the SALT I ceilings on numbers of missiles.
3. When, where, and by whom were the SALT II Agreements signed?
4. Give two reasons why some senators opposed SALT II, and two reasons why other senators supported it.
5. Explain one of the major ways the U.S. "verifies" that the U.S.S.R. is living up to arms control agreements.
6. In what month and year did the Soviets invade Afghanistan?
7. President Reagan created a commission to study whether there existed a "window of vulnerability." What did the commission decide?
8. What happened on June 12, 1982, in New York City?

8 Present Issues

Negotiations for a fifty percent cut?
What is "Star Wars" (SDI)?
What is the controversy around SDI?
What about Gorbachev and a new openness in the Soviet Union?

Although the United States and the Soviet Union did resume talking about the nuclear arms race, they made practically no progress. The talks were broken off, this time by the Soviets, and then resumed again. Even then, the two countries made hardly any progress.

Not until the autumn of 1986 did it seem that any real progress was being made. By the middle of 1987, there still had been no new *agreement*.

In some ways, the two countries are more ready today to reach an agreement—and an important one—than they have ever been. (See Figure 24.) But there is one major issue that at present divides them deeply. It may continue to divide them for some time to come.

This chapter is about how the two countries are dealing with the problem of the arms race today.

Figure 24 New agreements between the Soviet Union and the U.S. have raised hopes that peace will be maintained between these two heavily armed nations.

A FIFTY PERCENT CUT?

At the height of the peace movement in 1982 and 1983, a few experts suggested an idea they thought was better than the Freeze: instead of freezing, why not cut the number of weapons (or at least the strategic weapons) by half?

When this idea was first suggested, it seemed very radical. It was dismissed by most experts as too radical to take seriously.

President Reagan, however, said he approved of the general idea of "deep cuts" in strategic weapons. Gradually, the Soviet Union moved in this direction too. As the two countries continued talking, the idea of reducing strategic weapons by fifty percent came to seem more reasonable.

By the fall of 1986, the two countries reached a kind of understanding. *If* they could reach an agreement at all, that agreement would cut strategic weapons by half. This was, in a way, tremendous progress. Many people think that to some extent this progress resulted from the pressure of the anti-nuclear war movement. Before that movement appeared, the most that the two countries had discussed was setting numerical ceilings. The ceilings were as high, or higher, than the number of weapons each country already had. But by 1986 the U.S. and the U.S.S.R. were seriously discussing cutting the number of strategic weapons in half. As recently as 1982, no one would have predicted this.

The United States and the U.S.S.R., however, could not yet reach an actual agreement. One big issue, above all, divided them. To understand this you need to know about a new development.

A NEW RESEARCH PLAN: SDI

On March 23, 1983, President Reagan gave a very important speech. He said the time had come to try to find a defense against ICBMs and SLBMs. He expressed confidence in the ability of American scientists eventually to find a defense against these missiles. He said he would launch a big new research effort to achieve this.

President Reagan called this defense against ICBMs and SLBMs "a vision of the future that offers hope" and he made the following suggestion:

> . . . that we embark on a program to counter the awesome Soviet missile threat with measures that are

> defensive . . . What if free people could live secure in the knowledge that their security did not rest upon the threat of instant U.S. retaliation to deter a Soviet attack, that we could intercept and destroy strategic ballistic missiles before they reached our own soil or that of our allies?

In his speech, the president did not say what kind of defense he had in mind. In the days following Reagan's address, officials revealed that he was thinking of weapons in outer space.

President Reagan's speech took many top defense officials by surprise. The president had not checked with them beforehand about what he would say. This speech also received tremendous criticism. Many scientists who had been studying the problem of a defense against missiles were surprised. They said that there was no more reason now to think that a defense system was possible than there had been before.

Almost at once, President Reagan's idea got the name **Star Wars.** Because it involved weapons in outer space, it made people think of the movie 'Star Wars." The movie also came to mind because Reagan's idea involved *futuristic* weapons, not weapons for which technology already existed.

President Reagan and his advisors did not like the name "Star Wars" because they felt that made light of their idea. But "Star Wars" stuck.

President Reagan asked several groups of scientists to develop plans for the new research program, and he then created the program itself. He called it the "Strategic Defense Initiative," or **SDI** for short.

The President also created a new office in the

Pentagon to direct the SDI program. President Reagan set the research program's budget for the first five years at $26 billion.

The President and his advisors said that no decision would be made as to whether to actually *build* a system for intercepting missiles until the research had been done. They made it clear, however, that they thought a system *would* be built, perhaps in the 1990s.

Ever since its inception, SDI has been extremely controversial. Huge debates have raged among the experts and in Congress.

President Reagan asked Congress for large budgets for SDI. At first Congress responded. But by 1986 Congress began to cut back the funding. President Reagan and his advisors were not able to settle the controversy, and many experts told Congress that too much money was being spent too fast on SDI.

One of the reasons there has been so much argument about SDI is that President Reagan created a tremendous new hope, but many experts believe the hope is an illusion. President Reagan himself called it, at one point, his "dream."

The hope is that peace would not have to depend on deterrence anymore. If all ICBMs and SLBMs could be intercepted and destroyed before they reached the United States, then the U.S. would not have to threaten to retaliate if attacked. The U.S. wouldn't have to threaten at all. The U.S. would simply be safe behind an SDI "shield." That is what President Reagan suggested.

This idea sounds wonderful in theory. No one likes having to use deterrence to maintain peace, and of course everyone wants a solution to the danger of nuclear weapons and nuclear war. However, practically all experts say this kind of protection is impossible. At least it is impossible with any kind of technology that scientists know about now—or even know how to begin to research now. There are many reasons why, some of them very complicated; but two important reasons are fairly simple.

If the American people are going to feel really safe behind a "shield," then that "shield" has to work just about perfectly. But technology is never perfect. Most things break down sooner or later, or don't work quite right at first. This may be true even when engineers have worked very hard to design and build something extremely well. An example is the tragic explosion of the space shuttle *Challenger* in January 1986.

Suppose that the "shield" was able to stop ninety-eight percent of the attacking Soviet warheads. (By the way, even ninety-eight percent is much higher than scientists today know how to do.) That means two percent of the warheads would penetrate the shield. The Soviets have about ten thousand missile warheads, so two percent would be two hundred warheads. Two hundred warheads is enough to wipe out two hundred American cities!

You may have thought of the second reason already. The SDI program would create a "shield" only against ICBMs and SLBMs. But the Soviets also have bombers and cruise missiles. For these reasons and others, even most scientists in the Pentagon say privately that it's not possible, with any known technology, to build a reliable defense of the American people against nuclear weapons.

However, many experts believe that it's a good idea

to pursue research and development of advanced weapons like ones the SDI program is working on, in order to make technological progress. Some of these weapons might also help shield the underground silos in which the U.S. keeps its ICBMs.

PERSONALITY PROFILE:

Ronald W. Reagan

Ronald W. Reagan, (See Figure 25.) fortieth president of the United States, was born in 1911. He grew up and attended college in Illinois and worked for a while as a radio announcer in Iowa. When he was twenty-six he went to Hollywood and began a film career, which by its end in the 1960s had included roles in more than fifty movies. Often "Dutch" Reagan was cast as the second male lead. A famous line in the film *Knute Rockne, All American*—"Let's win this one for the gipper"—gave Reagan another of his nicknames. Reagan was also president of the Screen Actors Guild (the actors' labor union) for many years in the 1940s and 1950s.

Originally a New Deal liberal in his political outlook, Reagan moved rightward during those years, and by the late 1950s he was promoting a conservative philosophy as a TV spokesman for the General Electric Company. In 1964 he gave a smash speech in support of Barry Goldwater, the Republican candidate for President that year. The speech vaulted him

to national prominence, and after Goldwater's defeat conservatives began speaking of Reagan as an important political leader in his own right.

In 1966 Reagan ran for governor of California and defeated the incumbent governor by a huge margin. In the 1968 and 1972 presidential campaigns he threw his support to Richard Nixon, but in 1976 he decided to take on Gerald Ford, who had become president after Nixon resigned. Normally a sitting president wins his party's nomination easily, but Reagan came very close to wresting it away from Ford at the Republican national convention that year. In the 1980 Convention, Reagan won the nomination easily, and he went on to defeat Jimmy Carter in a landslide. When President Reagan campaigned in 1984 for a second term, his victory was even bigger.

SDI AND ARMS CONTROL

You remember that in 1972 the United States and the Soviet Union signed the ABM treaty as part of SALT I. The ABM Treaty forbids either country to build a defense against missiles. There is no time limit on this treaty; it is permanent.

This means that if the U.S. ever decided to build an SDI "shield," the United States would have to "tear up" the treaty. By ratifying the treaty, the U.S. Senate promised as solemnly as it can that the United States would not do that.

The one big issue that has divided the U.S. and the U.S.S.R. in the arms control talks of the last several years has been SDI. The Soviets have said that the SDI research program means that the U.S. plans to tear up the treaty in the future. The Soviets have said the U.S. must agree that SDI will *not* lead to anything that the treaty forbids. This means, to put it simply, that *research* is all right, but that the U.S. must promise not to *build* any kind of SDI "shield." President Reagan, however, has ordered the American officials talking with the Soviets not to promise this.

SDI is the main reason that the U.S. and the U.S.S.R. have not been able to reach a new arms control agreement. The Soviets say they will not sign any new agreement until the U.S. promises. President Reagan will not promise, because he wants to leave open the possibility of building an SDI shield in the future.

CHANGES IN THE SOVIET UNION

Recently, the Soviet Union has started to change rapidly, at least in some ways. In the spring of 1985 a new leader came to power in the U.S.S.R. His name is Mikhail Gorbachev.

Gorbachev is considerably younger than any Soviet leader in many years, and he has many new ideas for changing the way the Soviet system works. When he became general secretary, he immediately started putting his ideas into effect.

Many of the changes now occurring in the Soviet Union are very important and interesting in their own right, but they don't have a great deal to do with the arms race or arms control. Most of the changes revolve around **glasnost,** as it is called in Russian. *Glasnost* is usually translated as "openness." The changes that Gorbachev is making have introduced a kind of openness in the way that things are done, especially compared to the extremely rigid way things had been done in the Soviet Union before.

For example, the Soviet government is now talking with Western companies about "joint ventures," which would join Soviet and Western business enterprises. Gorbachev is also beginning to allow books to be published and plays staged about Joseph Stalin, General Secretary of the Soviet Communist Party, who ruled the Soviet union from 1922 to 1953. Stalin's tyranny was the most terrible time in the history of the Soviet government, and people in the U.S.S.R. were not previously allowed to read or write about it.

Although Gorbachev's changes are considerable, the Soviet system is not becoming "open" in the sense that an American would use the word. For instance, anyone in the Soviet Union can still lose his job simply for asking permission to leave the country, and the government almost never grants permission.

GORBACHEV AND ARMS CONTROL

Since Gorbachev became general secretary, he has made it very obvious that he wants arms control agreements. He has pushed the idea of a fifty percent cut in strategic weapons. He is also willing to yield in certain areas where previous Soviet leaders have been rigid. The most important of these is **inspection.**

You learned earlier that satellite "verification" by each country cannot always confirm completely that the other country is living up to arms control agreements. The best solution would be for American experts to go into the Soviet Union and see for themselves that the Soviets are "complying" (and for Soviet inspectors to come here). Many times in the past, the U.S. has asked for this right to send in inspectors.

Prior to Gorbachev, the Soviets always refused. With one or two minor exceptions, they refused *every time* the U.S. requested the right of inspection. Gorbachev has reversed this policy. He says he will allow inspectors to come in.

Defining in detail what inspection would mean is one of the main things that American and Soviet officials are talking about at present. Experts agree that if this can be worked out, it could be a tremendous breakthrough for arms control.

PERSONALITY PROFILE

Mikhail S. Gorbachev

Mikhail Sergeyevich Gorbachev (See Figure 26.) became the leader of the Soviet Union in March 1985. He is general secretary of the Communist Party, which means the Party's leader. Since the Party controls the government absolutely, the general secretary is the real head of the country.

Gorbachev came to power at the relatively young age of fifty-four, and since there is no fixed term of office nor age limit he might rule Russia for twenty years or more. However, he could be ousted if many of the other top leaders in the Soviet Union ever came to look on him as a failure.

A little like Jack Kennedy in 1960, Gorbachev entered office pledged to "get the country moving again." He had been immediately preceded by two elderly men (Andropov and Chernenko) who had held the supreme position only briefly, and before that by Brezhnev, who also had grown old in office and in his later years had launched little that was new. By the 1980s the Soviet economy was stagnating. Gorbachev knew it, and came to power determined to reinvigorate the Soviet system.

RECENT SUMMITS

Gorbachev and President Reagan have been meeting together in person. They have met twice recently and may meet again soon.

When the president and the general secretary meet in person, that meeting is called a **summit.** Since the late 1950s, a number of summit meetings have been held. Sometimes these summits helped in reaching a specific agreement and sometimes they didn't. Many people think it's a good idea for the president and general secretary to get together from time to time anyway, even if they achieve only a better understanding of each other as people.

President Reagan and General Secretary Gorbachev held their first summit in Geneva in November of 1985. A great many peace conferences and arms control talks have been held in Geneva, one of the major cities of Switzerland. At the Geneva summit, the two men talked mostly about arms control problems. (see Fig. 27.)

A little less than a year later, in October of 1986, the two men met again. This summit was held in Reykjavik, the capital city of Iceland. (The name of the city is pronounced RECK-ya-vik.) At the Reykjavik summit, the president and general secretary talked solely about arms control. They came very close to an agreement, but they were not able to reach one.

Figure 27 *President Reagan and General Secretary Gorbachev met at the Geneva Summit in November 1985.*

SUMMARY

President Reagan launched a new idea when he proposed in 1983 that American scientists try to find a way to intercept and destroy enemy ballistic missiles before they could reach the United States. Almost everyone finds this *idea* of a "shield" very attractive. But scientists say they don't know how a reliable, nearly perfect shield could be built. Some experts, however, support the "Strategic Defense Initiative" (SDI) as a way simply to explore technological possibilities and perhaps to shield our ICBM silos.

The Soviets claim that SDI means the U.S. plans to tear up the ABM Treaty. They will not make new arms control agreements until the U.S. promises not to do so—a promise that President Reagan has been unwilling to give. If and when a new agreement about strategic weapons can be reached, however, both sides say it will include a fifty percent cut.

Under their new leader, Mikhail Gorbachev, the Soviets have made concessions never made before, especially in allowing inspectors onto Soviet territory. What this may mean in practice is being discussed now.

REVIEW QUESTIONS

1. Why did the name "Star Wars" catch on as an unofficial name for the SDI program?
2. How much money, over how many years, does President Reagan plan to spend on SDI?
3. One reason that experts say a reliable "shield" against missiles cannot be built is that technology

cannot be made reliable enough. Give a famous recent example of a serious technological failure in the U.S.

4. What is a second reason why any "shield" we can presently design would not provide enough protection?
5. When did Mikhail Gorbachev come to power in the U.S.S.R.? What is the name of the top office there?
6. Give an example of *glasnost*.
7. A summit meeting was held in 1985 and again in 1986 between Ronald Reagan and Mikhail Gorbachev. What months were they held, and where?

9 Hope for the Future

What is the role of world public opinion?
What does "nonproliferation" mean, and why is it important?
What is the size of the U.S. and Soviet nuclear arsenals now?
Where are we headed?

The fact that General Secretary Gorbachev seems to really want new arms control agreements naturally makes many people feel hopeful for the future. Some experts feel that there may be more arms control successes in the next few years than have ever been seen before. They feel that the U.S. and the U.S.S.R. may be able to cut strategic weapons by fifty percent and then move on to other important steps. Other experts are not so sure.

In thinking about how the arms race and arms control might unfold over the coming years, another question should be considered. It raises both a possible problem and another reason to feel hope. That is the question of how other nations besides the U.S. and the U.S.S.R. deal with nuclear weapons.

PRESSURE FROM WORLD PUBLIC OPINION

The American and Soviet people are not the only people who worry about the nuclear arms race. So do many other people all around the world. In Europe, in Japan, and in every other place where people pay attention to international problems, people are concerned about the nuclear arms race. In recent years they have spoken out in a way they haven't before.

Of course, these people do not have nearly as much say in how decisions are made in the U.S. as Americans do, because only Americans elect the U.S. government.

But Americans and officials in Washington do listen, to some extent, to what people in other countries say. (The Soviet government listens to some extent also.) When large numbers of people all say the same thing, this has influence, especially when they keep saying it for a long time.

Some experts feel that "world public opinion" on the nuclear problem will become more significant as time passes. If more and more people around the world insist on halting the arms race, their weight will be felt.

THE NONPROLIFERATION TREATY

What nations other than the U.S. and the U.S.S.R. *do* also poses a possible problem for the future: **proliferation.** This word refers to the possibility that nuclear weapons might spread to more countries around the world and even might fall into the hands of terriorists. Already five countries besides the U.S.

and U.S.S.R. have nuclear weapons: Great Britain, France, China, Israel, and South Africa.

Experts long ago realized that it would be dangerous for more and more nations to have nuclear weapons. The more countries that have them, the greater the chance that somebody, someday, will decide to *use* some weapon.

This danger was already being studied in the 1960s, and soon American and Soviet officials were discussing it. In 1967 the two countries agreed to a treaty that they hoped would help solve the problem. To a large extent it has—but not completely.

The treaty is called the **Non-Proliferation Treaty.** The United States and Soviet Union jointly asked every nation to sign it. Under the treaty, every nation that signs it agrees that it will never acquire nuclear weapons. (In exchange for this, that nation can receive help from the U.S. or U.S.S.R. in building nuclear reactors for electrical power.)

Over a hundred nations around the world have signed the Non-Proliferation Treaty by now. Unfortunately, a few countries refused. It will not surprise you to learn that the ones that refused are the very countries that experts suspect *want* to obtain nuclear weapons.

Israel refused, as did South Africa. So did India, Pakistan, Argentina, Brazil, and several others.

THE AMERICAN AND SOVIET WEAPONS

As of today, both the U.S. and the U.S.S.R. have about twenty-five thousand nuclear weapons each, for a grand total of fifty thousand. Of these, each country has about ten thousand "strategic" weapons.

The other fifteen thousand or so are on military ships at sea, or they are artillery shells or short-range missiles for each side's army and air force.

Some people feel that this large a number is ridiculous. After all, it would take only a couple hundred nuclear weapons—at most—to bring either the United States or the U.S.S.R. to an end as a functioning nation. These people use the word "overkill" to describe this situation.

Some experts, however, do not believe that this number of weapons should be called **overkill.** These experts say that not all the weapons would be used in any one war, and that each country needs to prepare for many possible kinds of war.

THREE IDEAS FOR THE FUTURE

As we come to the end of this book, we will look at three ideas of what may happen or should happen in the future. Each one of these ideas is supported and believed by many Americans. Now that you know something about the arms race, you can decide what you believe.

Of course, each person has his or her own specific ideas about the future, but most ideas fall into one of these three categories. (There is no single accepted name for any of these, so we will describe them.)

AN INEVITABLE ARMS RACE?

One idea for the future is that the arms race between the U. S. and the Soviet Union is pretty much inevitable. It has been going on for forty years now and it will continue.

People who believe this usually think that arms control can make some difference in the *way* the arms race unfolds, but it can't *stop* the arms race.

People who think that the arms race is inevitable sometimes call themselves "realists." They feel it is only realistic to believe that the arms race will inevitably continue.

"Realists" in the U.S. are skeptical about the Soviet Union. They suspect that the Soviets want to expand their power more and more. If Gorbachev is talking about arms control, these people say, it's because he wants to use it to gain advantages for the Soviet Union.

The "realists" feel that the Soviets will build more and more weapons and new weapons to build up their power. So to keep the Soviets at bay, the United States will also have to build more weapons and new weapons. That is why the arms race won't stop.

One problem with this idea is that it doesn't seem to offer very much hope. But people who believe it say that this idea pretty well describes the history of the last forty years, and there is no reason to expect any basic change.

A TECHNOLOGICAL SOLUTION?

Another idea for the future is that if the United States tries hard enough, the U.S. can find a technological solution to the arms race. We can find a weapon so powerful that the Soviets just won't be able to do anything about it.

A good example of this idea is President Reagan's vision of SDI. President Reagan says that if American scientists are given time and enough money, they can invent a "shield" that will simply keep out all missiles. (Perhaps another shield can also keep out bombers and cruise missiles.)

If shields such as these could be invented then the United States would be safe from nuclear war. Even if the Soviets attacked, their weapons wouldn't get through.

One problem with this idea is that for many years, Soviet scientists have been only a little behind American scientists in inventing new weapons. Anything we can build, they can find a way to counter. But people who do support this theory say American scientists are the best, and if they haven't discovered the right thing yet, they will.

A POLITICAL SOLUTION?

A third idea of the future is that the United States and the Soviet Union can reach understandings that will halt the arms race and reduce the danger. No doubt it will have to be done step by step, but it can be done.

People who believe this idea believe in working hard on arms control and on improving our relationship with the Soviet Union. If we can achieve better relations, we can learn to understand each other better (and vice versa).

Proponents of this approach don't believe the Soviets want to take over the world; or if they once did, they have learned that they're not going to succeed, and they've given up trying. People who think this also think that the Soviets are afraid of nuclear war, just as we are. So they *want* to find a solution.

Creating new understandings and agreements is

something that experts might call a "political" solution. Some people might call it a "human" solution.

One problem with this idea is that it really does depend on the Soviets not wanting to expand their power more and more. Suppose they do? They could pretend to go along with the United States for a while, and then when the U.S. stopped watching them carefully, suddenly leap ahead. But people who believe this third idea say that in the process of reaching understandings we actually would be getting to know them (and so in a way "watching" them) more, not less.

WHICH FUTURE?

Now that you have learned something about these problems, you can make up your own mind. What do *you* think?

GLOSSARY

ABM The acronym for Anti-Ballistic Missile. A missile, or in some definitions, any weapon intended to shoot down ICBMs and SLBMs.

air defense system A system of radars, computers, missiles, and other elements intended to shoot down attacking aircraft.

arms control Efforts to slow down and halt the arms race, and to put limits on, or reduce, the numbers of weapons. More generally, "arms control" also includes other means for reducing the probability of a nuclear war occurring, such as the Hot Line.

arms race A continuing competition between two or more nations for more weapons or more advanced weapons.

assured destruction capability A government's certainty that its military forces are capable of destroying another country. For example, the U. S. government's certainty that U. S. military forces can destroy the Soviet Union.

atomic monopoly A situation where only one nation on earth has nuclear weapons. The U. S. had an atomic monopoly from 1945 to 1949.

Cold War The name given, beginning in 1947, to the state of high tension and hostility between the U.S.S.R. and the Western democracies.

conventional weapons Weapons that are not nuclear.

cruise missile A missile which flies horizontally within the atmosphere, like an airplane.

deterrence Preventing an attack by an enemy nation by convincing that nation's leaders that the destruction of their nation would suffer in consequence would be too great. (This is the usual meaning. In military usage, "deterrence" can also mean a threat to deny the enemy any opportunity to meet his objectives; for example, a threat to successfully defend the border, so his attacking army will be thrown back.)

fallout Dust and other tiny particles, sucked up into the upper atmosphere and made radioactive by a nuclear explosion. This material then falls out of the atmosphere over days, weeks, or years.

first-strike capability Not the capacity to strike first, but the capacity to strike first so successfully that the enemy cannot make an effective counterattack.

glasnost A Russian word usually translated as "openness." Mikhail Gorbachev uses this word to describe a series of reforms he hopes to make in the Soviet system.

ICBM Inter-Continental Ballistic Missile.

inspection With regard to arms control, sending people into another nation's territory to verify that the nation is doing what it has committed itself to do.

kiloton A measure equal to a thousand tons of the explosive chemical TNT. This is another measure of the power of a nuclear explosion.

MAD Mutual Assured Destruction. Mutual deterrence between two nations, each of which has an "assured destruction capability" against the other.

MIRVs Multiple, Independently targetable Re-entry Vehicles.

missile A rocket that carries a bomb.

mutual deterrence Two nations each of which is preventing attack by the other by "deterrence" (see above), are together employing "mutual deterrence."

NATO North Atlantic Treaty Organization: the alliance among the U.S., Canada, and twelve Western European nations.

Non-Proliferation Treaty A treaty, signed by more than one hundred nations by now, outlawing the transfer of nuclear weapons, or the means of making them, to nations that do not yet have them.

overkill A word some people use to describe a situation of more than fifty thousand nuclear weapons in the world.

parity Rough equality in numbers of weapons.

proliferation With regard to arms control, the process by which nuclear weapons spread to nations (or groups) that previously did not have them.

puppet government A national government that follows the instructions of another nation and is sustained in power by that other nation.

ratification In the United States, the formal, legal approval of a Treaty by the U.S. Senate.

Red Army The army of the Soviet Union.

retaliation To retaliate is to strike back after having been attacked.

SALT The acronym for Strategic Arms Limitation Talks.

SDI Strategic Defense Initiative. A program begun by the Reagan Administration to research possible new weapons for defending the U.S. against attack by ICBMs or SLBMs.

secure weapons Weapons that cannot be successfully attacked.

SLBM Submarine-Launched Ballistic Missile.

stable deterrence A situation of mutual deterrence between two nations that lasts over time because small changes in the numbers or types of either side's weapons cannot upset the basic balance.

Star Wars A name for SDI often used by the public.

strategic In the context of nuclear weapons, "strategic" weapons are weapons, based either at sea or in one country's homeland, that can reach an enemy's homeland.

summit A meeting between two or more heads of state.

verification With regard to arms control, determining that the other side is actually doing what it has committed itself to do.

warhead A small bomb carried by a missile.

window of vulnerability A belief held by some Americans in the late 1970s and early 1980s that there would be a period of time during which U.S. ICBMs would be vulnerable to Soviet attack.

BIBLIOGRAPHY

Articles

Ball, George. "The War for Star Wars." *New York Review of Books,* June 1985, 38–44.

Bethe, Hans A., and Robert S. McNamara. "Reducing the Risk of Nuclear War."*Atlantic Monthly,* July 1985, 43–51.

Harvard Nuclear Study Group. "The Realities of Arms Control: A Primer for Laymen." *Atlantic Monthly,* June 1983, 39–49.

Krauthammer, Charles. "The Real Way to Prevent Nuclear War." *New Republic,* April 28, 1982.

———. "The Illusion of Star Wars." *New Republic,* May 14, 1984, 13–17.

Nitze, Paul. "SDI: Its Nature and Rationale." *Current Policy* No. 751 (1985).

Norris, R. S., et al. "History of the Nuclear Stockpile." *Bulletin of the Atomic Scientists,* August 1985, 106–09.

Pipes, Richard. "Why the Soviet Union Thinks It Could Fight and Win a Nuclear War." *Commentary,* July 1977.

Powers, Thomas. "Nuclear Winter and Nuclear Strategy." *Atlantic Monthly,* January 1984, 35–50.

Rostow, Eugene. "Why the Soviets Want an Arms Control Agreement, and Why They Want It Now." *Commentary,* February 1987, 19–26.

Sagan, Carl. "Nuclear War and Climactic Catastrophe: Some Policy Implications." *Foreign Affairs* 62 (1983–84): 257–92.

Books

Allison, Graham T., Albert Carnesale, and Joseph S. Nye, Jr., eds. *Hawks, Doves and Owls: An Agenda for Avoiding*

Nuclear War. New York: W. W. Norton and Company, Inc. 1985.

Blacker, Coit D., and Gloria Duffy. *International Arms Control: Issues and Agreements*. Stanford: Stanford University Press, 1984.

Boutwell, Jeffrey, Donald Hafner, and Franklin A. Long, eds. *Weapons in Space*. New York: W. W. Norton and Company, Inc., 1986.

Bracken, Paul. *The Command and Control of Nuclear Forces*. New Haven: Yale University Press, 1983.

Carter, Ashton B., and David N. Schwartz, eds. *Ballistic Missile Defense*. Washington, D.C.: Brookings, 1984.

Cohen, Stephen F. *Sovieticus*. New York: W. W. Norton and Company, Inc., 1985.

Dyson, Freeman. *Weapons and Hope*. New York: Harper and Row, 1984.

English, Robert D., and Jonathan J. Halperin. eds. *The Other Side: How Soviets and Americans Perceive Each Other*. New Brunswick, N.J.: Transaction Books, 1987.

Fallows, James. *National Defense*. New York: Random House, 1981.

Freedman, Lawrence. *The Evolution of Nuclear Strategy*. New York: Random House, 1981.

Halloway, David. *The Soviet Union and the Arms Race*. New Haven: Yale University Press, 1983.

Hersey, John. *Hiroshima*. New York: Bantam Books, 1946.

Jastrow, Robert. *How to Make Nuclear Weapons Obsolete*. Boston: Little, Brown, 1985.

Jungk, Robert. *Brighter Than a Thousand Suns*. New York: Harcourt Brace Jovanovich, 1958.

Lehman, John F., and Seymour Weiss. *Beyond the SALT II Failure*. New York: Praeger, 1981.

Lifton, Robert J. *Death in Life: Survivors of Hiroshima*. New York: Vintage Books, 1967.

Luttwak, Edward N. *The Grand Strategy of the Soviet Union*. New York: St. Martin's Press, 1983.

McNamara, Robert S. *Blundering into Disaster*. New York: Pantheon Books, 1986.

Nacht, Michael. *The Age of Vulnerability*. Washington, D.C.: Brookings, 1985.

National Academy of Sciences. *Nuclear Arms Control: Background and Issues*. Washington, D.C.: National Academy Press, 1985.

National Conference of Catholic Bishops. *The Challenge of Peace: God's Promise and Our Response*. Washington, D.C.: U.S. Catholic Conference, 1983.

Newhouse, John. *Cold Dawn: The Story of SALT.* New York: Holt, 1973.

Pipes, Richard. *Survival is Not Enough*. New York: Simon and Schuster, 1984.

Schell, Jonathan. *The Fate of the Earth*. New York: Alfred A. Knopf, 1982.

Smoke, Richard. *National Security and the Nuclear Dilemma: An Introduction to the American Experience, 2d ed.* New York: Random House, 1987.

Sommer, Marc. *Beyond the Bomb: Living Without Nuclear Weapons*. Massachusetts: Expro Press, 1985.

Spector, Leonard S. *Going Nuclear*. Cambridge, Mass.: Ballinger Publishing Company, 1987.

Talbott, Strobe. *Endgame*. New York: Harper and Row, 1979.

———. *Deadly Gambits*. New York: Alfred A. Knopf, 1984.

Union of Concerned Scientists. *The Fallacy of Star Wars*. New York: Vintage Press, 1984.

United States Arms Control and Disarmament Agency. *Arms Control and Disarmament Agreements*. New Brunswick, N.J.: Transaction Books, 1984.

Ury, William. *Beyond the Hotline: How Can We Prevent the Crisis That Might Bring On a Nuclear War*. Boston: Houghton Mifflin, 1985.

INDEX